Praise for Michael Seely's *Turning Point*

Motivated by love of country and his Millennial children, Mike Seely's book is a sobering statement of the present status of our nation's problems and the burden they place on our children and grandchildren. Much of what you see here should make you want to get involved!

—U.S. Senator Connie Mack III (Fla.; Ret.)

Seely has done the impossible thing with this book; he has made engaging reading out of America's trajectory toward economic doom. His diagnosis is utterly convincing and it is impossible to read Seely's book and not admit that the fortunes of the next generation are hostage to those who came before them and have been living high by running up debts their kids will be stuck with. But Seely also prescribes solutions and they do not, mercifully, seem beyond the country's capabilities. Only, so far, its will. Perhaps this book will be a wake-up call as well as a compelling read.

—Geoffrey Norman, author and columnist
(*Wall Street Journal, The Weekly Standard*, et al.)

Whether or not you embrace all of Michael Seely's candid advice to Millennials, he masterfully spells out the recurring historical patterns and urgent financial concerns the new generation must confront today.

—Stephen W. Quickel, editor of *US Investment Report*,
former senior editor of *Forbes*,
and managing editor of *Institutional Investor*

Mike Seely tells it like it is. The future will be less secure for millions of Americans unless we get our national house in order. Turning Point dispels myths and offers a roadmap to prosperity. We must summon the courage to follow it. This is a must-read for Millennials first and foremost, but really for all of us who care about our kids and grandkids.

—Jim Douglas, four-term governor of Vermont
and former chairman, National Governors Association

What a scary reality that Michael Seely is brave enough to point out to the world. This is a seminal book that Millennials must read to park their sense of entitlement and focus on the numerous problems now facing their generation, and Baby Boomers must digest to face the harsh reality of the world they have left for their children. It's not too late to implement the changes suggested here, but the countdown clock is ticking.

—Jim Kim, founder and general partner at Formation 8

An excellent, sometimes humorous, always insightful recap of Left/Right, socialist/capitalist perils and pitfalls during the past half-century. Directed toward the Millennials, who Seely argues have already paid dearly for the mistakes of the Baby Boomers, Turning Point expresses hope for America's future—if young people wake up to the "right" way. His take on the last 50 years of Vermont politics is a compelling harbinger of what could be in store for the nation itself, and his deft integration of insights from Pulitzer Prize-winning playwright David Mamet's The Secret Knowledge is fascinating.

—Tim Butler, founder/managing partner, MeritBSC

Michael Seely

Michael Seely founded and ran a management consulting firm, an investment partnership, and chaired HSBC's mutual fund group. His previous work includes books on maximizing shareholder value and corporate restructuring. Mike has contributed to the major business and financial publications and lectured at leading business schools. After retiring to Vermont in 2002, he served briefly—and with an utter lack of distinction—as finance chair of the state's Republican Party. He lives in Vermont, Florida (naturally) and the Caribbean.

TURNING POINT

Saving our kids' future.
And our own.

Michael Seely

SHIRES ❧ PRESS

Manchester, Vermont

SHIRES ✿ PRESS

4869 Main Street
P.O. Box 2200
Manchester Center, VT 05255
www.northshire.com

©2015 by Michael Seely

ISBN:
978-0-692-46478-6

Building Community, One Book at a Time

Printed in the United States of America

For my two millennials, Mike, Jr. and Luke,
and for the love of my life, Meg—
together, an embarrassment of riches.

Acknowledgements

My cheerleader on this project has been Geoffrey Norman, a pro with almost twenty books and countless other literary work under his belt, popular *Wall Street Journal* and *Weekly Standard* contributor, and all-around good guy. Thanks, brother.

Were it not for the ongoing contrast between my ultra Democratic friends in Vermont and my Republicans friends in Florida (not to mention my socialist and Ganja Party friends in St. Lucia), I might never have bothered. But you convinced me there must be a better way—and that we better damn well find it pretty soon. Thanks to all of you, too.

Alex Lajoux, a friend since her days as editor of *Mergers & Acquisitions*, and an author herself, has been a big help—with research, fact-checking, occasional editing and spirit-boosting. How do I say thanks?

Much gratitude is reserved for my friends who read early drafts—Peg Gregory, John McClaughry, Alex Mentes, Tulley Mott, Cook Neilson, Mike Rollyson, Tom Stevenson and many others. You can now hopefully see just how helpful your comments have proved to be. For the cover design I'm in debt to my friend and Dartmouth classmate, John Talbott, and for the overall book design to David Williams and Becky Holcombe.

Finally, I am grateful most of all to my wonderful wife. Writing is a lonely job in some ways, but a selfish one as well, perhaps necessarily. She remained a saint through it all—which means, she was always in character.

Needless to say, any errors or omissions are the author's fault. Of which he has many.

Contents

Foreword

I raised two of you Millennials—one is now 35, the other 33—and love them both very much. Wrote a lot of checks, put 'em through school, got their teeth fixed—you know the list. But what they didn't know was that I had my hand in their pockets the whole time. That's what we've done to our kids—mortgaged their future to pay for our own.

Today, properly accounted for, every man, woman and child in the United States is in hock for almost $700,000. We Boomers will die without having to pay it all back; but Millennials won't. We can't keep kicking the can down the road anymore; the numbers are too big and the promises are too governing.

And it isn't just an American problem. All around the world, we see mountains of debt—and mountains more of government obligations. The Great Recession had a singular result—through bailouts and quantitative easing, we socialized (i.e., passed to the government and hence taxpayers) a mountain of private debt. But the debt is still there.

We Boomers stood by, absorbed in our own lives, jobs, concerns, while we mortgaged *your* future. Worst of all, we Boomers too-often bought into that most nefarious of lies: "We're from the government and we're here to help you." We naively believed the government actually could!

First, we cut taxes and ran up the government debt to astronomical levels. Now we're raising your taxes to pay for our benefits. Those benefits—Social Security, Medicare, you know the list—are relatively secure for us in the short-run. That explains why you hear precious few complaints today. But you will.

To the extent we noticed it at all, we blithely accepted our central bank's "dual mandate"—fight inflation and maintain "full" employment—and their presumed ability to temper the normal ups and downs of the business cycle. Wrong.

The pollsters tell us you Millennials don't expect to see any of this largess that we have garnered for ourselves. That's good—because you probably won't.

But you *will* get the bill.

So to my apology, let me add, "thank you."

Your parents and I tolerated feckless politicians and we kept voting for them even when they did little but compound the problems we now face.

And we allowed our attention to be diverted a hundred times from the issues that truly matter—the issues that lead to economic growth and rising abundance for all. We went for "nice" and neglected "smart." In the end, most of us came finally to appreciate what creates opportunity, equality, and justice—and to realize that the government usually only gets in the way.

Now we're reaching a turning point—or so history implies. Most societies crumble when national debt and government commitments reach these levels—and, in other words, when civic virtue declines. The end of Pax Americana—more than two centuries of success as the greatest nation on earth save, perhaps, for Rome or Great Britain—is drawing near.

We live now in a world where governments are struggling to cut debt, their effort stymied by slow growth and bad demographics. Hence, they must make the debt easier to live with by reducing their borrowing costs and regulations that encourage banks to stuff their vaults with government bonds. Martin Barnes, Chief Economist at The Bank Credit Analyst, calls this "financial repression."

Several things could save us.

- Technology will help—new medical breakthroughs *could* cut overall healthcare costs, for example, but don't count on Silicon Valley. And it is certainly cheaper and cheaper to have many nice things like PCs and iphones.
- Baby Boomers *could* wake up tomorrow nourished by a new sense of selflessness and willingness to sacrifice and, of course, change their views on distracting issues to focus on those that foster growth. But that's unlikely.
- Politicians *could* wake up tomorrow as statesmen; quite unlikely as well.

- We *could* all wake up tomorrow with a newfound ability to distinguish between the explicit and hidden messages our public servants send our way. I doubt that, too. We're too dumb, they're too clever or both.
- Looking at America's huge debt burden, and the increasing possibility of civil unrest down the road, the markets *could* throw in the towel and crash, crushing the economy and finally focusing us on what truly matters.
- In short, the Long Hustle is coming to an end.

You Millennials are the folks with skin in the game, big skin—and a central premise of this book is that the outcome is in your hands.

I know who you are. To the extent you pay attention to politics and social issues, you are frustrated. You care about the latter, sometimes passionately, but feel a mild sense of disgust about the first. You're liberal on the social issues—often fervently so—but increasingly conservative on the economic ones, for good reason.

I know it's hard to reach you by conventional means—the databases don't capture you because you move a lot. You stream video so we can't reach you via cable and the like. And when we do get to you, you often turn off and then you tune out.

I know something else. You're waking up to what we did to you. A few of you are starting to focus and understand that your generation could experience a near cataclysmic decline in your standard of living—you see signs of it already, and the big move isn't far away.

The intention of this book is modest—to put before you and your parents, my peers, some people and perspective on what I perceive to be the issues that matter. Here you will find some of the most devoted citizens in America—and some of the smartest. Any one of the issues we will take up could consume volumes, so think of this as a survey.

My life has taught me that free markets work better than government bureaucrats. I am data-driven, and I've also learned that as data changes so too must our views. Change is never easy. Consider the lifting the toilet seat talk ... or asking directions ... you know. So, I've also included some analysis on how views are formed and how they may change—on those odd occasions when fresh information suggests that they should.

I've also included some advice on your personal finances and the like. That's how I've spent most of my life and, after all, you're going to need all the help you can get.

Visit our website, www.tinfl.org (for "There is no free lunch").

Get involved.

Do the work—these issues are complex, but they have never mattered more.

We can't let the politicians set the discussion agenda for us—we must set it. And we must hold them accountable. The time to start is NOW, as we build to the 2016 election.

And don't ever forget—we, especially you Millennials, *can* save America.

We're living on borrowed time today, so for everyone's sake, we'd better try.

Good luck. America is still the best hope for mankind. Don't ever forget that.

Enjoy the read.

TURNING POINT

PART ONE

We've Got a Very Big Problem

CHAPTER 1

This Canyon Has Very High Walls

In the economic box canyon where we find ourselves, our choices are limited and our prospects appear grim. America will soon be unable to fund government's many extravagant and irresponsible promises or to any longer steal from the young who were crippled by the recession. Increasing financial obligations and bad policies increasingly thwart opportunity-expanding growth—our only way out.

Many intrepid settlers of the American West died gruesome deaths after they rode into a so-called "box canyon". Once inside, the hostile Indians sealed the entrance—the settlers' only egress—and so the settlers' fate as well. So, too, it appears to be in America. We've ridden into a financial/economic box canyon—one with near-vertical walls that seem impossible to scale. It's killing our kids' futures and now threatens our own as well.

Imagine you are opening your mail one morning. You come finally to an official-looking envelope that says "U.S. Government—VERY IMPORTANT." Your pulse quickening, you open the envelope and begin scanning the text and tables on the page before you, your eye moving quickly to the bottom of the table where you see, "Total due"; then, your jaw drops as you read "Due Federal Government: $56,000."

"My God," you think, "how did THAT happen?"

Okay—relax. The government is too sneaky to be that direct with us.

But the number—and the obligation—are real. As we go to press with this book the level of debt per person is $56,000—and we can't repay it because for the first time, it's more than what we are producing per person. U.S. gross domestic product per capita is lower than U.S. federal debt per capita. And that's bad news.

In fact, if you bring up the web site of the U.S. Treasury (www.treasury. gov), you can see what the IOU number is per person at this exact moment.

You Owe Uncle Sam a Lot of Money

But this picture is profoundly misleading. It doesn't reflect the "off balance" sheet obligations—promises like Medicare and Social Security, among others. Many others. Add these up, discount them to present value, make some reasonable assumptions about future tax revenues, and that $56,000 rises to almost $700,000 for every man, woman and child in the U.S.!

The "give/get" is pretty simple: we Boomers—at least for a while—are the "get", you Millennials are the "give".

This book is about how that happened—about the real and peripheral issues that divide us—and about what we can (indeed, must) do about it.

Just a few years ago, the picture was very different. In fact, the Congressional Budget Office predicted that government budget surpluses would get bigger and bigger, amounting to almost $6 trillion between 2002 and 2011—enough to pay off all the federal debt!

That didn't happen; au contraire. In fact, we added $6 trillion to the debt—which is now some $18 trillion (including some $5 trillion in "intergovernmental" holdings) according to the U.S. Treasury.

So what happened?

Where did those surpluses go?

Most importantly, a really bad recession intervened—the worst since the Depression. That explains $3.3 trillion. Add tax cuts—another $2.8 trillion. "Nation-building" in Afghanistan and Iraq ($1.2 trillion), post-9/11 Homeland Security outlays, President Bush's new prescription drug benefit ($275 billion in 2011 alone), TARP ($500 billion, but mostly repaid), and a bigger interest bill on rising debt ($1.4 trillion), and you see the picture.

This book is also about government perfidy. Some of the specific sources of it are open to debate, depending on how partisan you might be and how much you want to argue about politics instead of parsing recent history for understanding, always hard-won. There's plenty of irresponsible and self-serving bad behavior around so that no one is without guilt. And, most important of all, the crisis facing our country goes way beyond the Boomers and the Millennials—*everyone is threatened.*

And in the end it's our own fault. We keep asking for more from government while we complain more bitterly about the bill. Until now, we could just pass it on to our kids, but those days will soon be over—the numbers are simply too big.

Those born after 1980, the Millennials, are almost irretrievably disadvantaged—relative to their parents, for sure—due to the inimical and disproportionate effects on them, and their younger brethren as well, of the Great Recession. The Great Recession simply showed us all how bad things can be—and will get—if we don't act now. And those consequences were most bitterly imposed on America's young.

While many financial commentators are excited by gains in payrolls, the news isn't so great for Millennials. Those of employment age born in the early 1980s and afterward account for 40 percent of the unemployed, or 4.6 million people, according to a study from the Georgetown University Center on Education and the Workforce which was provided to *MarketWatch*. That total compares to 37 percent, or 4.2 million, for Generation X, and 23 percent, or 2.5 million, for Baby Boomers. Generation X consists of people born from 1965 to 1980. Baby Boomers are those born from 1946 to 1964.

"I was surprised by how high that number is for Millennials," Andrew Hanson, a research analyst at Georgetown University who analyzed the data, told *MarketWatch*. "Unemployment is becoming a youth problem."

Of the 4.6 million jobless Millennials, two million have been out of work for at least six months.

We see the harbingers of this already.

- In 1990, youth unemployment in the United States was 11 percent; now according to the U.S. Department of Labor it's more than 14 percent overall. And it's even higher for Hispanics (16.5 percent) and blacks (24.8 percent).

  In addition to unemployment of the young, there is their underemployment—a pervasive shortfall between potential and accomplishment.

- First and foremost, there are those disheartened young job-seekers who've forsaken their search or who are working only part time. That group is currently at 15 percent, according to Gallup polls.
- But there is a subtler and more pervasive kind of underemployment for the young—when recent college graduates settle for jobs that don't require degrees. In 2012, says a study from the New York Fed, 44 percent of recent college grads under the age of 27 were underemployed in this qualitative sense—compared to 33 percent overall.

A Generation Forever Scarred by Recession

Not surprisingly, Millennial wages are depressed. The most recent Census and statistical abstracts bring us more bad news: the average salary of young college graduates has dropped 15 percent, about $10,000, since 2000.

According to Heidi Shierholz, a labor economist who follows youth employment for the Economic Policy Institute, "It's never been this bad." For 2011 and 2012 graduates, a 19 percent pay cut from what they might have had without the recession was the norm, according to economists at Yale—about twice the penalty of prior recessions.

The long-term consequences of this misfortune will prove profound and enduring. The lower wages that come from entering the job market during a recession, or "wage scarring", will haunt recent graduates for years, Shierholz notes. Earnings shortfalls have persisted for a decade and a half, University of Maryland researcher Shu Lin Wee has found, attributing this to the fact that half of all income gains achieved between 18 and 46 occur by age 30 as workers switch jobs to improve their lot. By way of example, I started out in 1967 working in the complaint department of American Express' new credit card division; I was paid $7,000 a year. Five job switches and 10 years later, I was the assistant treasurer of the 63rd biggest company in the U.S. and making 10 times that. It was easy then; it's almost impossible now.

Student Debt Obscures the Real Issue

And growing college debt worsens the situation. In 1992, when tuition averaged $16,000, students borrowed a total of $26.4 billion for college; in 2012, with tuition almost doubling to more than $30,000, they needed $110.3 billion, up four times.

This pushed total student loans to $1.2 trillion—much of it delinquent or in default, foreclosing tens of thousands of young people from home ownership and obliging them to defer marriage.

Elizabeth Warren—Student Loan Crusader and Classic Redistributionist

First-term Senator Elizabeth Warren of Massachusetts is alarmed about the rising cost of higher education and student debt, and wants to do something about it (well—about the loan part anyway).

She proposes to cut the interest rate on these loans to less than 4 percent and finance that cut with a tax on America's top earners. She also wants to provide a refinancing option, so borrowers can take advantage of declines in prevailing market rates.

But, she told *Rolling Stone*, "Unfortunately, the federal government can't just reduce the interest rate. It has already built those expected profits into the budget. So we propose stitching up tax loopholes that are available only to millionaires and billionaires."

Buying this? Hear anything about lowering the fast-inflating cost of education?

Disadvantaged though they may be, much will by necessity be asked of Millennials. To understand why, look at demographic trends in the U.S. and what they portend. The key takeaway is this—a perfect demographic storm is upon us. Just as millions of Baby Boomers sign up for Medicare and draw their first Social Security checks, the still working young whose paychecks get docked to pay those bills, are shrinking as part of our population. Thus, fewer and fewer workers will be available to fund a bigger and bigger bill for the entitlement programs. This relationship between "give" and "get" is what economists term a *dependency* ratio—and ours is not just bad; it's awful. In 1950, there were 16 workers per Social Security recipient, but by 2033 there will be just 2.1 workers.

As the Willie Nelson song goes, "it's not supposed to be this way." Henry Hazlitt put it even better in *Economics in One Lesson*:

"The original Federal Social Security Act was passed in 1935. The theory behind it was that the greater part of the relief problem was that people did not save in their working years, and so,

when they were too old to work, they found themselves without resources. This problem could be solved, it was thought, if
they were compelled to insure themselves, with employers also
compelled to contribute half the necessary premiums, so that
they would have a pension sufficient to retire on at sixty-five or
over. Social Security was to be an entirely self-financed insurance
plan based on strict actuarial principles. A reserve fund was to
be set up sufficient to meet future claims and payments as they
fell due.

"It never worked out that way. The reserve fund existed mainly
on paper. The government spent the Social Security tax receipts,
as they came in. ... Since 1957 current benefit payments have exceeded the system's tax receipts."

Al Gore and His Mythical Lockbox

In a masterful sleight of political hand that combined two deceptions
in one heartfelt pledge, candidate Al Gore—the self-proclaimed inventor
of the Internet—promised in his 2000 campaign to put the Social Security
trust funds in a "lock box" to assure that they'd be there for future beneficiaries. Lie No. 1—there is no trust fund; it doesn't really exist—it's just a
pile of government IOUs. Lie No. 2, in corporate cash management, where
treasurers electronically "sweep" their business units and consolidate
excess working capital in a so-called "lock box" (i.e., any secure location)
from whence the funds can be invested short-term to earn some return,
those funds are in and out of the lock box in an instant. This is just the
opposite of Mr. Gore's intended point.

While the long-term implications of a slow-growing working population and a rapidly expanding older population are sobering for younger
Americans, they are certainly worrisome for the rest of us, too.

For fiscal 2014, which ended October 1, 2014, the Federal budget
showed approximately $3 trillion for receipts and about $3.5 trillion for
expenditures, giving us a deficit for that year alone of nearly $500 billion.
(Of course, we don't usually have a real budget. But that's another story.) Of
that $3 trillion, more than half goes for so-called entitlements—including
Social Security, Medicare and Medicaid (an estimated $814 billion, $586
billion, and $450 billion, respectively, says the Congressional Budget
Office). (By contrast, the outlays associated with our military activities

around the world, most notably Iraq and Afghanistan, consumed only $578 billion in fiscal 2014.)

As Baby Boomers Retire, the Burden on Social Security is Growing Enormous

The intent, and willingness, to provide for our aging citizens is laudable. And many of them need our help. Many elderly Americans (a total of 58 million in 2014; nine out of 10 over 65, get a check every month) rely on Social Security; half of married couples and 75 percent of singles get at least half their retirement income from Social Security.

The story is the same with government healthcare entitlements—the federal program, Medicare (created in 1965), and the state-federal program for the poor, Medicaid (created by the same legislation).

As pointed out in the Cato Institute *Handbook for Policy Makers*, Medicare was founded on the "morally suspect and impractical premise" that "government should tax young workers to pay for the healthcare needs of their elders, many of whom do not need it and many of whom never contributed to the program."

Medicare and Social Security are linked—give up Medicare and you forfeit your Social Security benefit.

A Deteriorating Dependency Ratio

Like most entitlement programs, Medicare has a powerful constituency and politicians happily reward these voters with ever more generous enhancements to the program—all of which come with a cost, most recently Medicare Part D, the prescription drug benefit proposed by President Bush and enacted by Congress in 2003, to solid applause from the pharmaceutical industry, for whom it dramatically boosted demand overnight.

Like Social Security, spiraling costs put the healthcare programs in jeopardy as well. Medicare's own trustees predict that the ratio of workers paying for it and beneficiaries—four workers per beneficiary in 2003—will decline to 2.4 in 2030 and only two in 2078. This is called a dependency ratio and ours is deteriorating badly.

Wondering how we're going to honor all these commitments? I'll let you in on a dirty little secret.

The money isn't there.

That's where you come in, Millennial.

CHAPTER 2

Don't Expect the Cavalry to Save Us

Still believe "We're from the government and we're here to help you?" The government is the biggest culprit behind most of our ills. Abetted by the doomsayers, always with us, they wring their hands and purse their lips on a wide range of social and economic issues from climate change, income redistribution, population growth, and technology. But, they are often barking up the wrong tree. Despite all the other demands on our time, we really have to pay attention now and focus on what really matters.

I trace my political awakening to cancer. Until I was diagnosed with advanced colon cancer, I didn't pay much attention to public policy. Adult life as a self-employed businessman and single parent left little time for ruminations about such things. So I missed how the American dream was being remorselessly compromised by countless bad public policy decisions by feckless politicians, aided by apathetic voters … of which I had been a prime example.

Midway through successful treatment (thank you, Memorial Sloan Kettering), in 2002, I shuttered my businesses and moved from Greenwich, CT, my home for almost three decades, back to Vermont, where I'd attended high school, but which I'd left in 1963.

With time on my hands now, I looked around at the state I'd left forty years before—then a low-tax citadel of self-reliance and individualism—and saw a vastly different environment. Vermont, land of cows and maple syrup, had become what the entire U.S. is becoming—and for similar reasons.

THE GREEN MOUNTAIN STATE GOES BLUE

Where once it had been stolidly Republican, with a nearly unbroken stream of Republican Governors from its earliest days to 1963, Vermont voted consistently Democratic now.

- Its Washington representatives were among the most liberal of any state, and included Senator and presidential aspirant Bernie Sanders, who describes himself as a socialist and acts like one;
- It was among the most highly taxed states in the U.S., and
- Among the worst states by several polls in which to do business.

Figure 1: Growth States vs. Declining States

RANK	STATE	RANK	STATE	RANK	STATE
1	Utah	18	Alaska	35	Nebraska
2	South Dakota	19	Tennessee	36	Hawaii
3	Indiana	20	Alabama	37	New Mexico
4	North Dakota	21	Oklahoma	38	Washington
5	Idaho	22	Colorado	39	Kentucky
6	North Carolina	23	Ohio	40	Maine
7	Arizona	24	Missouri	41	Rhode Island
8	Nevada	25	Iowa	42	Oregon
9	Georgia	26	Arkansas	43	Montana
10	Wyoming	27	Delaware	44	Connecticut
11	Virginia	28	Massachusetts	45	New Jersey
12	Michigan	29	Louisiana	46	Minnesota
13	Texas	30	West Virginia	47	California
14	Mississippi	31	South Carolina	48	Illinois
15	Kansas	32	New Hampshire	49	Vermont
16	Florida	33	Pennsylvania	50	New York
17	Wisconsin	34	Maryland		

- School spending is the biggest item in the Vermont state budget, as it is in most other states; it has risen by high single digits each year, while the school population declines by small single digits and, by all measures of educational attainment, the results do not change.

And today the situation is even worse. Vermont ranked No. 5 for highest taxes in 2013, and by some calculations, is No. 1 today. Worse yet, the ALEC-Laffer State Economic Competitiveness Index (from the American Legislative Exchange Council, with economist Arthur Laffer) ranked the Green Mountain state No. 49 for economic outlook (see chart above). Only New York, with its crushing tax burden, did worse.

WHAT HAPPENED? AND WHY DOES IT MATTER?

It matters because Vermont is the canary in the coal mine—the chirping bird that by dying warns the miners of the poisonous gas, so they may escape. Vermont is a harbinger of what is in the offing for America if things don't change.

As to what happened—that's a somewhat longer tale.

David Mamet, the powerful Pulitzer Prize-winning playwright ("Glengarry Glen Ross") and director, attended college in Vermont (ultra-left Goddard College, Plainfield, Vt.) when this political metamorphosis was occurring in Vermont. He traced his intellectual journey from liberal to conservative in *The Secret Knowledge: On the Dismantling of American Culture.* We quote him throughout this volume because he offers a fascinating and unique interior glimpse of a deeply-thoughtful person's political evolution—a journey that many of us make. And many more should.

> "My question, then, was that as we cannot live without government, how must we deal with those who will be inclined to abuse it—the politicians and their manipulators? The answer to that question, I realized, was attempted in the U.S. Constitution—a document based not upon the philosophic assumption that people are basically good, but on the tragic confession of the opposite view. ... The great wickedness of Liberalism, I saw, was those who devise the ever-new State Utopias, whether crooks or fools, set out to bankrupt and restrict, not themselves, but others. ... I saw that I had been living in a state of ignorance, accepting an unexamined illusion and calling it 'compassion', but that there were those brave enough to work their way through the prevailing slogans of their time, and reason toward a consistent, practicable understanding

of human relations. To these, politics was not the manipulation of the ignorant and undecided, but the dedication to the defense and implementation of just, first principles, for example, those of the United States Constitution. ... I saw that to proclaim these beliefs in individual freedom, in individual liberty, and in the refusal to blindly surrender all powers to the State, was, in the general population, difficult, and in the Liberal environment, literally impossible, but yet men and women of courage devoted their lives and energies to doing so, deterred neither by scorn nor its inner twin, despair.*

* "The Right and the Left, I saw, differ not about programs, but about goals—the goal of the Left is a Government-run country and that of the Right the freedom of the individual from Government. These goals are difficult to reconcile, as the Left cannot be brought either to actually state its intentions, or to honestly evaluate the results of its actions."

—David Mamet, *The Secret Knowledge*

During the "back to the earth" movement in the Sixties, when Mamet was at Goddard College, tens of thousands of hippies and others made Vermont their home. Overrun by these idealistic young voters, the pendulum swung far away from traditional Vermont values. With the passing of time, those lacking trust funds or unusual success at weaving or organic farming or pottery, returned to their origins, leaving their better-funded liberal brethren behind.

Social Experimentation on a Low Budget

A second factor also played a role. Vermont is a small state—only 625,000 citizens, of whom only 193,500, or less than half, cast ballots in the 2014 elections; hence, it is easy for any group with an issue to press to reach this electorate. And they do. Vermont has recently received money, for example, from George Soros to encourage a statewide single-payer healthcare system (more on this later).

So in many ways, Vermont is an inviting test tube for those pressing social experimentation and is thus a sometime harbinger of the national political scene. You often "see it here first" because it's cheaper here to get the issue in play. Rather than feel patronized by these out-of-state "social scientists", Vermont seems flattered to submit to their experiments.

For example, Vermont passed the first GMO labeling laws last year. Two other states voted down GMO labeling in the recent midterm elections; it seems likely, however, that this will become a national issue (though the FDA has already ruled that GMO food is safe). More, too, on this a little later.

The Catastrophist Canon Has Cost Many Lives

Before setting out to elaborate on it, these new, post-hippie Vermont voters bought the "catastrophist" canon of the Seventies and Eighties. In it, we see the antecedents to today's fractious debates on peripheral issues like new drilling technology and GMOs.

Rachel Carson's *Silent Spring*, first published in 1962, warned of a spring without chirping birds as DDT (dichloro-diphenl-trichlorothane, whose inventor, Hermann Muller, won a Nobel in 1948 for its discovery) and other pesticides imperiled our wildlife and children (this although DDT has never been directly linked to a single human death). It accused the chemical industry, abetted by their political allies, of spreading disinformation about pesticide use and attributed tens of millions of needless deaths to their use.

Though the author did not herself call for a ban on DDT use, it certainly led to one and spawned the environmental movement, which in turn led to the creation of the U.S. Environmental Protection Agency on December 4, 1970, when it was born as a full-blown bureaucracy with some 20 guaranteed senior titles—including a full-time job for a Director, Equal Opportunity—and five central offices and 10 regional offices—all from day one, and it has only grown since that day.

The EPA banned DDT in 1972; thereafter neither the U.S. nor UN would fund its use in Third World countries. Bear in mind that hundreds of thousands, mostly young children, die every year of malaria, which the pesticide would certainly temper, if not eradicate, were its use not discouraged or outlawed.

The result of that ban? A lot of blood on a lot of hands. It's worth looking closely at how that ban occurred because it's instructive of how truly dangerous government bureaucrats can be.

AND THERE GOES THE GOVERNMENT AGAIN

Mark Levin captures the sordid truth behind the costly DDT ban in *Liberty And Tyranny*:

> "... even the manner in which the EPA banned DDT was an abuse of both scientific and legal process. An EPA administrative law judge held several months of hearings on DDT's environmental and health risks. In the end, Judge Edmund Sweeney found that 'DDT is not a carcinogenic hazard to man. ... DDT is not a mutagenic or teratogenic hazard to man. ... The uses of DDT under the regulations involved here do not have a deleterious effect on freshwater fish, estuarine organisms, wild birds or other wildlife.'
>
> "However, Sweeney's ruling was rejected by EPA administrator William Doyle Ruckelshaus (Author's Note: who enjoyed a highly successful subsequent career), who, in 1972, banned it anyway. Ruckelshaus attended none of the hearings and aides reported he had not read the hearing transcript before overruling Sweeney's findings. At the time, Ruckelshaus belonged to the Audubon Society and later joined the Environmental Defense Fund, which, along with the Sierra Club, was a budding organization that brought lawsuits pressing for the DDT ban."

Overall, the ban has resulted in the deaths of millions. And the carnage continues every year.

The Population Bomb, suggested by the then Executive Director of the Sierra Club, was the second piece of the catastrophist canon—a 1968 publication by Stanford University professor Paul Ehrlich—which forecast a world of mass starvation where hundreds of millions perished in the 1970s and '80s as an exponentially expanding world population eclipsed the earth's ability to feed it. Erlich saw no solution but urged bringing the population growth to zero or less (precisely the problem in several parts of Europe today), even mass sterilization.

These prophets of doom are unrepentant. Robert Bryce in *Smaller Faster Lighter Denser Cheaper* notes that 45 years after the publication of *The Population Bomb*, Paul Ehrlich "was still pushing his claim that we are facing a catastrophe. In an interview in *Forbes*, Ehrlich was asked what he might say to President Barack Obama if given the chance. Ehrlich replied that Obama "should lead the world in showing that economic growth is the disease, not the cure, and shift focus to equity and gross national happiness."

BILL MCKIBBEN—VERMONT'S VERY OWN CLIMATE CATRASTROPHIST

Ditto Bill McKibben of 350.org and one of America's prominent environmentalists, who argues against nuclear power and natural gas—though they offer the only near-term option relative to coal.

McKibben is lionized by the Left. A Vermont resident and ubiquitous presence at the debate about energy, global warming, and how to "save our planet", he is fond of challenging those with whom he disagrees to "do the math".

Well, Robert Bryce does just that in *Smaller Faster Lighter Denser Cheaper*, when he takes on McKibben, using McKibben's own math.

In his 2010 book, *Earth: Making a Life on a Tough New Planet*, McKibben argues that to "stabilize the planet" and reduce the atmospheric concentration of carbon dioxide to 350 parts per million, then "we need to cut our fossil fuel use by a factor of twenty over the next few decades."

But hear Bryce's retort: "In 2011, the average resident of planet earth consumed about 4.9 liters (1.3 gallons) of oil-equivalent energy per day from hydrocarbons. Therefore, if McKibben's plan were enacted, each of the seven billion residents of the planet would be allowed a daily ration of hydrocarbons that "wouldn't fill an average-size soda can."

"On a ration of one liter of gasoline per day, a Prius driver in the U.S. would be limited to no more than 13 miles of driving per day. The driver of a Chevrolet Suburban would be allotted about four miles a day," Bryce continues.

"The bottom line here is obvious: if the countries of the world decided to embrace McKibben's anti-nuclear, anti-hydrocarbon proposals, the result would be dire poverty for billions of people around the world.

McKibben may couch his rhetoric in environmental terms," Bryce concludes, "but his proposals are a prescription for economic suicide."

Even the head of the Sierra Club, Michael Brune, "has shown his catastrophist credentials," Bryce reports. "Rather than embracing natural gas as a way toward cleaner air and lower carbon dioxide emissions, he's begun calling natural gas an 'extreme fossil fuel'. Brune claims that gas is 'a gangplank to a destabilized climate and an impoverished economy.'" No matter that the rationalists can marshal considerable factual evidence to the contrary.

The Limits to the Club of Rome's Capacity to Think

The Club of Rome is another player in this catastrophe club. Founded in 1968 as an association of self-described "independent leading personalities from politics, business and science, men and women who are long-term thinkers interested in contributing in a systemic interdisciplinary and holistic manner to a better world," it came into prominence in 1972 with its best-seller, *The Limits To Growth*, which sold to some 12 million people in 37 languages the idea that the world would soon close in on itself. Subsequent editions of that book (most recently in 2004) softened the predictions but like the notion of the imminent end of the world promoted by various religions, the notion lingers. Today, the Club of Rome is a well-funded Utopian "think tank" and is currently "focusing ... on the root causes of the systemic crisis by defining and communicating the need for, the vision and the elements of a new economy, which produces real wealth and well-being; which does not degrade our natural resources and provides meaningful jobs and sufficient income for all people."

These and other inputs coalesced Vermont's '60s hippies' innate concern for their world, and their sense of their own important role in improving it, into what might be called an attitude of "narcissistic altruism."

This narcissism persists. Vermont's leftist governor, recently reelected by the thinnest of margins, likes to cite the state's apparently enviable employment situation, but he dissembles. He cites Vermont's low unemployment rate—among the nation's lowest, he says, but what Gov. Shumlin doesn't say is why. As Vermont's *Burlington Free Press* recently noted,

> "There just aren't a lot of people out there for businesses (or government or non-profits) to hire. That shows up in the statistics

as a low unemployment rate with little or no job growth. Which is exactly what we are seeing."

Compare this record to that of North Dakota, a state much like Vermont in population size and other factors, which from October 2013 to October 2014 (before the oil price rout) alone added 22,500 new jobs (to be sure, many of them shale oil—and necessarily "fracking"-related; Vermont's legislature banned fracking in the state—though no oil and gas company has ever expressed any interest in seeking energy in the Green Mountains). By contrast, Vermont is losing jobs—and population—as those who can do so desert the state for lower-tax, higher opportunity states.

So Vermont matters more for what it portends for America than for what it is.

There is no secret to why great societies fail—it comes down to bad policy, sometimes wedded to good (though misguided) intentions. It was as true of ancient Rome or Great Britain as it is of our growing number of failed American cities. Examples abound, but none are more compelling and sorrowful than that of Detroit, once the vibrant citadel of American manufacturing. Nobody describes its downfall better than Charlie LeDuff.

Detroit—A Harbinger of Things to Come?

"I believe that Detroit is America's city. It was in the vanguard on the way up, just as it is in the vanguard on our way down. ... Detroit is Pax Americana. The birthplace of mass production, the automobile, the cement road, the refrigerator, frozen peas, high-paid blue-collar jobs, home ownership and credit on a mass scale. America's way of life was built here.

"It is where installment purchasing on a large scale was invented in 1919 by General Motors to sell their cars. It was called the Arsenal of Democracy in the 1940s, the place where war machines were made to stop the march of fascism.

"Once the nation's richest big city, Detroit is now its poorest. It is the country's illiteracy and dropout capital, where children must leave their books at school and bring toilet paper from home. It is the unemployment capital, where half the adult population does not work at a consistent job. There are firemen with no boots, cops with no cars, teachers with no pencils, city council members with telephones tapped by the FBI, and too many grandmothers with no tears left to give.

"But Detroit can no longer be ignored, because what happened here is happening out there. Neighborhoods from Phoenix to Los Angeles to Miami are blighted with empty houses and people with idle hands. ...

"Go ahead and laugh at Detroit. Because you are laughing at yourself."

—Charlie LeDuff, Detroit, An American Autopsy

You see in Vermont's present circumstances the same things that marked the early days of Detroit's tragic decline: high taxes, over-regulation and employment declines, with a profoundly irresponsible approach to financing adoption of a highly liberal agenda.

VERMONT VS. NEW HAMPSHIRE: A STUDY IN CONTRASTS

Currently, Vermont's economic growth rate is flat at 2 percent. This is a sharp contrast with the 1960–1980s, when Vermont grew at double-digit rates. But these growth rates were diminished by a series of taxpayer- and employer-unfriendly steps.

- In the '70s, the state began to assess a land-gain sales tax on property acquired and quickly subdivided. This "anti-land flipping" law is still on the books.
- Its income tax rate rose steadily and now starts at 8.95 percent for those in the highest bracket.
- Vermont is among the few states with an estate tax. The paperwork starts for those receiving as little as $600 (yes, that's right, 600 dollars) and it applies to some out-of-state payments as well.
- The sales tax is 6 percent statewide, with some municipalities exacting an additional 1 percent, probably in the middle of the pack nationally.
- But, if your income is $90,000 or below, you get a property tax break (though this must obviously shift the burden to those residents whose incomes are more than $90,000). And there's an even bigger break for those earning $47,000 or less (more wealth transfer). Half of Vermonters get a property tax rebate.

In addition to its proximity to greater Boston, however, New Hampshire has no land gain tax, no tax on wages, no estate tax and no sales tax.

Guess which state has the faster-growing economy, population and incomes? If you guessed New Hampshire, you're right.

And, as you might expect, Vermont features enough regulations of every variety to drive a sane person mad. Just consider this example.

Enough to Drive a Man from Drink

Kenny Felis is a serial entrepreneur who loves Vermont. With just one little catch.

But, let him tell you.

"I decided to make ice cider—'hard' cider, if you will.

"I hired a good lawyer to line up my permits—state and federal since we're dealing with alcohol here. Got 'em—no problem. But then we learned that those permits covered making the product; I needed a 'solicitor's permit' to sell it. And I couldn't take the product into a store—it had to stay in the winery (Forbidden Orchards LLC, Colchester, Vt.). Oh, and the store must pay cash—we can't extend credit or sell on consignment.

"Farmers' markets are very popular in Vermont since we have a strong 'buy local' culture here. A logical place to preview our product. But we learned we needed to get a 'farmers market' permit—one for each different farmers' market. And if we wanted to offer consumers a taste of the cider or sell it to them, we needed a 'tasting' permit. To quality for this, our fourth permit, we needed to complete a state course to learn how to identify under-age drinkers. In fact, we must re-take the course every two years in case we forget something. If one of our employees leaves our company, but stays in the industry, he must retake the course, even if he took it a month before!

"Of course, the state charges fees for all of this."

Still Wonder Why Vermont is the Fourth-Worst State for Small Business?

What does a regulatory climate like Vermont's suggest? A close parallel to bankrupt Detroit and Greece. In what *Wall Street Journal* columnist Bret Stephens describes as his "stool sample story", he describes how some Greek entrepreneurs—reminiscent of my friend Ken Felis—tried to set up an online business specializing in organic olive oil products. First, they needed the right paperwork, which required authorizations from the government tax office, the local municipality, the fire department, and the bank, which insisted that their entire web site (this was to be an online business) be in Greek and only Greek—despite their intent to market internationally. Finally, the health department stipulated that shareholders have chest X-rays and submit stool samples.

It took the founder 10 months to thread this maze.

How long might it have taken in Vermont?

Vermont and New Hampshire both have large state legislatures which meet annually: Vermont's numbers 180, New Hampshire's 424—but with a big difference. Vermont pays its solons $10,000 a year, more (if your party is in power) for "summer studies", plus expenses; New Hampshire legislators get $100 a year plus expenses (if they live more than 50 miles from Concord, the capitol). The difference clearly finances a lot of mischief.

Bad Tax Policies and the Shadow Economy

I spent a lot of time in Argentina in the Seventies—the time of the *desaparecidos* ("disappeared ones"—in many ways that country's equivalent of our Vietnam War-opposing hippies). An economist could trace Argentina's ills (then AND now) to horrific public policies—then it was deeply protectionist trade policies (not unlike our Smoot-Hawley tariffs) on which time finally ran out, and the domestic unrest that flowed from them. That, unfortunately did not help the desaparecidos, who, as much as the pathology of Argentina's military, were victims of corrupt economic policy. The junta who ran Argentina at the time were paranoid about the left which led to unprecedented repression and some of the most atrocious crimes against humanity ever committed in this hemisphere. Many of those young people were kidnapped, tortured and then dumped from Argentine Air Force planes—sometimes with their stomachs slashed open—into the Atlantic outside Buenos Aires.

In odd counterpoint, movie attendance was very high. And nothing on the screen was as amusing to Argentines as when—sort of like our old pre-feature cartoons which we no longer see—they screened film clips from the government urging all good Argentines to pay their taxes. Laughter cascaded through the theater, for this is a nation where tax cheating is a bigger national pastime than soccer. And soccer is BIG.

And Who Could Blame Them?
It's Coming Soon to a Theater Near Us.

When we lose respect for something, we devalue it in many ways—e.g., if we perceive taxes as unfair, or the use to which they are put as wasteful or purposeless, we seek ways not to pay them.

Even today, in America, the cash or "underground economy" is where you go to make a—shall we say, "discreet"—living. It includes the mafia (or what's left of it), to whom the allure of tax-free income is often how law enforcement puts them away (convicted of tax cheating rather than murder or extortion), as well as your favorite server at the local bar and grill. Anyone, in fact, who fails to report income is a member of this large and growing community. And Vermont's high-tax economy is rife with cash-based employment.

It is notoriously difficult to get hard facts about tax compliance—for obvious reasons. But based on anecdote it is high and rising in places like Vermont and other high-tax northern states, where more and more people at moving into livelihoods where workers are paid in (undetectable—by the IRS) cash.

Show Biz and Millennial Role Models

The story of Vermont, with instructive parallels and contrasts around the country and the world, would not be complete without the mention of the Woodstock concert of 1969 and the polemical culture it launched. In advertising "three days of peace and music," and featuring anti-war songs, the concert had an agenda beyond entertainment: it was to change the world, like the social experimenters who infiltrate the Green Mountain state today. To be sure, the original concert occurred in New York (in the town of Bethel, as a matter of fact), but Vermont's own town of that name has given similar concerts with a cause. As these young Baby Boomers, whether in Vermont or elsewhere, continued to champion a variety of social causes, their pursuit was abetted by a new set of troubadours—Bruce Springsteen, Bob Dylan—as well as well-intended, but politically- and economically-naive show business personalities and athletes.

There are ironies here. While Dylan might decry the one who "dressed so fine, threw bums a dime", and "used to ride on the chrome horse with your diplomat/Who carried on his shoulder a Siamese cat," he vacationed on a 250-ft. yacht in the Caribbean. And The Boss would sing of the "mansion on the hill" from the perspective of a poor kid gaping at wealth, but he actually bought mansions in Florida for millions.

The list of showbiz idealists is long. Jason Mattera notes in his book *Hollywood Hypocrites*:

> "Hollywood hypocrites are the perfect embodiment of all that is wrong with the Left's ideas and policies. Not only do progressive positions fail, but also they are so bankrupt that even their loudest adherents live lives that stand in direct opposition to their ideology.
>
> "Michael Moore blasts capitalism and the profit motive ... then sidesteps hiring union members to cut costs, demands full payment from studios, and maximizes every inch of existing tax laws to squeeze every last dime of profit he can out of his movies.
>
> "Sting and Trudie Styler lecture us common folk on our need to repent from our carbon-spewing ways ... then hop their private jet, with their massive concert trailer trucks in tow, and hopscotch around the globe lugging their 750-person entourage and leave a Sasquatch-sized carbon footprint in their wake.
>
> "Arianna Huffington writes best-selling books denouncing the 'pigs at the trough' whose appetite for greed and profit destroys the rights and livelihoods of workers ... then turns around and pulls off one of the shrewdest media mergers in recent memory by converting the free labor of nine thousand bloggers into a $100 million payday for herself.
>
> "Bono travels the globe shaking down nations who are in debt to hand over even more of taxpayers' hard-earned money in the name of African 'debt relief' ... then plays a shell game with his band's corporate structure to avoid paying higher taxes—the very same taxes that would otherwise be used for, well, African debt relief.
>
> "Matt Damon holds forth on the corrosive effects of violence in media ... then makes movies wherein he brandishes weapons and kills people with his bare hands if necessary to make fat bank at the box office.
>
> "The point isn't that Michael Moore shouldn't maximize profits, Sting and Trudie Styler shouldn't travel, Arianna Huffington shouldn't be hard-nosed in business, Bono shouldn't be as tax-efficient as possible. Quite the contrary! The point is that these and

the scores of celebrities I've exposed throughout this book advocate that the heavy and crushing hand of government denies us the very liberties that they use to catapult themselves to prosperity and stardom.

"And that's the point: since progressives see government as the solution to every social ill, the Left's hypocrisies bring with them a unique danger, because they carry with them the oppressive weight of governmental laws that control human behaviors and limit freedoms."

When they were younger, the Boomers bought into some very misleading role models as well, and, partly as a result, some false views of how the world works. One thing they got right—and we have the calamitous war in Vietnam to thank for this—was that the government can be tragically inept on an epic scale. How else can you describe a war that cost 59,000 young Americans their lives? We didn't "make the world safe for democracy"; we helped companies like Nike with their global supply chain, since Nike now routinely sources their sneakers there.

Dogged Myths That Persist and Bedevil Us Still

The government has proven itself remarkably adept at ducking accountability for its actions. For example, the Great Depression is commonly ascribed to the stock market crash of 1929—a symbol of capitalist greed; today's demagogues blame a greedy Wall Street for the recent Great Recession, attributing no responsibility to government and its all-out push to boost housing at any cost. In fact, most forensic economists now see that 1929 crash as a mere symptom of the problem. They ascribe the depth and duration of the economic agony of the 1930s to poorly conceived government actions, going back to the Smoot-Hawley Tariff of 1930, which raised U.S. tariffs on 20,000 imported goods and set off a global trade war.

"This is the vision of FDR, who elaborated a bad economic downturn into the worst depression in history. In an attempt to Do Good for All, he dismantled the free market, and, so, the economy and saddled our country not only with 'social programs', but with the deeper, unconscious legacy of belief in Social Programs, irrespective of their effectiveness. Roosevelt's great domestic bequest was this syllogism: If anything called a Social Program fails, expand it."

—David Mamet, *The Secret Knowledge*

Similarly, the Great Recession, from which we are just now emerging, is commonly blamed on Wall Street and the Big Banks; in fact, one may convincingly argue that it was the government's actions to "democratize" housing that led banks to degrade their mortgage lending standards. This was one of the many conclusions in the then-minority (Republican) report at the end of the 600-plus page *Final Report of the National Commission on the Causes of the Financial and Economic Crisis in the United States*, published in January 2011. Also leading to the catastrophe, and noticed by the minority report: the government's "implied" support to Fannie and Freddie, so-called "government sponsored entities" or GSEs, that induced (some would say *coerced*—through legislation like the Community Reinvestment Act) the financial world to package and distribute the resulting bonds into commingled products like CMOs (collateralized—i.e., by the bonds—*mortgage* obligations; CDO refers to other forms of debt). Along the way, government regulators tragically and myopically overlooked the profound conflicts of interest at the rating agencies, which got paid to evaluate the very bond vehicles they drew fees for helping to design!

(Author's Note: In early 2014, Standard & Poor's settled government allegations that it inflated its mortgage-backed investment ratings and paid $1.5 billion. It did not admit fraud, nor were any of its officers or directors indicted for fraud. Moody's, another rating agency, which arguably followed similar business practices, went unpunished.)

Most recently, and most ironically, the banks are being fined billions of dollars for doing precisely what government bureaucrats, regulators, and politicians demanded of them—to make housing affordable to millions of Americans, despite their lack of creditworthiness. That the government compelled some institutions to acquire other, troubled institutions, which they had themselves failed to adequately supervise, then fined the acquirers for the sins of the acquirees is even more bitterly ironic. But it does deflect responsibility from the government and ascribe it to the private sector—inspiring the "Occupy Wall Street" and other movements, not to mention the anti-Wall Street rhetoric that is a staple of populist orthodoxy.

Most galling of all—two of the most aggressive politicians on boosting housing and lowering lending standards to do it, Barney Frank and Chris Dodd, have their names firmly affixed to a financial "reform" bill that has done absolutely nothing to remedy "too big to fail", while entrenching a mammoth new bureaucracy. Among many other destructive provisions, the law requires that banks claw back any pay they have awarded to executives or directors who are later deemed (by the government, of course) to be "responsible" for insolvency. For such bankers, it's a terrible life—the opposite of the wonderful Jimmy Stewart movie in which a small town banker in hard times receives money from his appreciative community.

And therein lies one of our central points—the paradox of so many good intentions. Put another way, if you think the government is here to help you, you must love the song lyric, "you always hurt the one you love" because that is what so many of these policies do.

And there is a reason for it.

The best explanation of well-intentioned policies that have this paradoxically bad result is the dispersion of their cost and the concentration of their benefit. It also explains the powerful role of special interest groups. And why, despite the heavy burden the results place on all of us, so many of us are indifferent to public policy and the painfully repetitive nature of public policy failure.

Rainy Day Lament: 'Where Are the Damn Cabs?'

Ask any New Yorker why it's so hard to get a cab on a rainy day. Be prepared for profanity. But, Milton Friedman can tell you.

Turns out, there's a reason. New York's Taxi and Limousine Commission limits the number of medallions. No medallion, no cab. These medallions, which recently traded hands at $872,000 each under downward pressure from Uber (more later), have topped $1 million in price—and there are only 13,437 of them, their number tightly regulated by said Commission. This constitutes a very high barrier to entry to all those who might wish to ferry us around—high, but not insurmountable as shown by the abundance of so-called "gypsy" drivers, especially during peak times (think of Broadway 10 minutes after the curtains close).

One can speculate about how many additional drivers might be induced to enter the trade were the entry barriers not so high. This would, most likely, lead to better service on rainy days and even lower fares. But it hasn't happened.

Why not?

Concentrated benefit and dispersed cost, according to Friedman. Try to change the system and the cab owners—who make campaign contributions and enjoy access—complain bitterly to the Mayor, who out of sympathy might even raise rates. And so the rest of us (who don't know who precisely to blame on those rainy days) pay even more for those few cabs we can hail.

And this is how public policy gets made.

FREE MARKETS ÜBER ALLES?

Enter Uber. The Uber app, on your phone, will show you a map with available drivers and how long it will take them to get to you. It estimates the cost of the ride, names the driver, and gives you his phone number and license. The ride gets billed to your credit card—with a receipt showing the route you took, time and average speed. Amazing. THIS is what Schumpeter meant by creative destruction—in this case, of the entrenched medallion-cossetted cab system.

No wonder Uber meets fierce opposition everywhere it goes: Washington, D.C., New York (where the aforementioned New York Taxi and Limousine Commission holds sway and has lobbied to put Uber out of business on the dubious pretext that it discriminates against the elderly), even Germany and France (where cabbies in Paris smashed windows and slashed tires of Uber vehicles), and virtually every other foreign market the company enters.

In his classic 1993 monograph, published by the Hoover Institution, *Why Government is the Problem*, Milton Friedman noted that:

> "The major social problems of the United States—deteriorating education, lawlessness and crime, homelessness, the collapse of family values, the crisis in medical care—have been produced by well-intended actions of government. That is easy to document. The difficult task is understanding why government is the problem. The power of special interests arising from the concentrated benefits of most government actions and their dispersed costs is only part of the answer. A more fundamental part is the difference

between the self-interest of individuals when they are engaged in the private sector and the self-interest of the same individuals when they are engaged by the government sector."

And it keeps happening, despite our occasional passion about an individual issue about which we may each feel strongly.

All this serves to remind us of the essential nature of neurotic behavior: doing the same thing and expecting the outcome to change.

Well, things aren't changing. They're going from bad to worse. Much worse.

Wander back over recent years and try to find a government success story. Warning us of 9/11? The Boston Marathon bombers? How about the VA hospital mess? Healthcare.gov? The General Motors ignition switch? Bernie Madoff? Prevention of the Financial Crisis of 2008–2009 by the securities watchdogs? No success stories here. In fact, unbelievably, at least 33 Securities and Exchange Commission employees—most of them paid in the six figures—viewed hours of porn on SEC computers during the recent financial crisis, accelerating a habit that was already ingrained, as the SEC's own inspector general attested in a report prepared at the request of Sen. Charles Grassley (R-Iowa), a man known for his ability to expose government waste—very much in the tradition of the late Sen. William Proxmire (D-Wis.).

No wonder the slacker's well-worn dismissal of a quality breakdown: "close enough for government work."

We can't fairly ascribe problems or solutions to one political party or the other. In the words of Laurence Kotlikoff and Scott Burns, authors of *The Coming Generational Storm*:

> "... is one political party more honest than the other when it comes to disclosing the mess we're handing to our kids? No. Each party has its constituents, all of whom share the convenient property of being alive and being able to vote. Future kids don't have that luxury, and current kids are kept far away from the polling booths. So the goal becomes to make the grown-ups happy. The Democratic grown-ups are happy when the government spends more money (on them). The Republican grown-ups are happy when the government raises less taxes (from them). The ideal

solution, then, is to spend more and tax less."

One of the ironies (in the way it incentivizes private citizens to do what bureaucrats get paid to do) of the aforementioned Dodd-Frank law is the money it lavishes on whistleblowers against the private sector. The whistleblower gets a cut of 10 to 30 percent if he or she makes a report that leads to a sanction of $1 million or more. And the jobs of whistleblowers—even those whose claims do not pan out—are protected under anti-retaliation provisions in this law and its precursor, Sarbanes-Oxley.

Pity Paul O'Neill, but Be Thankful for His Example

Yet by way of additional example of the "one standard for us, another standard for you" tradition of government, it's clear that truth-tellers in government assume considerable risk; if you aren't a "team player", you can get fired and the truth has nothing to do with it. One example is that of Paul O'Neill, former Secretary of the Treasury under George W. Bush, but there are others—David Stockman, author of *The Great Deformation* (2013, Penguin Books), was fired as Ronald Reagan's budget director following candid remarks to the press.

O'Neill's fate is especially contemptible.

> "If anyone would listen to him, Paul O'Neill thought, Dick Cheney would. The two had served together during the Ford Administration, and now as the Treasury Secretary fought a losing battle against another round of tax cuts, he figured that his longtime colleague would give him a hearing.
>
> "O'Neill had been preaching that a fiscal crisis was looming and more tax cuts would exacerbate it. But others in the White House saw a chance to capitalize on the historic Republican congressional gains in the 2002 elections. Surely, Cheney would not be so smug. He would hear O'Neill out. In an economic meeting in the Vice President's office, O'Neill started pitching, describing how the numbers showed that growing budget deficits threatened the economy. Cheney cut him off. 'Reagan proved deficits don't matter,' he said. O'Neill was too dumbfounded to respond. Cheney continued: 'We won the midterms. This is our due.'

"A month later, Paul O'Neill was fired, ending the rocky two-year tenure of Bush's first Treasury Secretary, who became known for his candid statements and the controversies that followed them. Rarely had a person who spoke so freely been embedded so high in an Administration that valued frank public remarks so little."

—John F. Dickerson, "Confessions of a White House Insider", *Time* magazine, January 2004

THE BIG ONE IS STILL OUT THERE

Many would like to think the Great Recession is over and the moment of great economic peril is behind us. Not in my view. Baby Boomers may well die before the Next Big One. But we may not. And you Millennials remain at significant risk of an even bigger upheaval.

- The global financial imbalances are simply too big and the lack of clear vision too obvious.
- Public/financial policy options have grown very limited. Even so-called "Quantitative Easing" has been disparaged by former Fed chairman Ben Bernanke. ("It works well in practice, but not in theory.")

What is assured is that unless something changes, today's young will almost certainly be the first generation in American history to have a lifestyle worse than the previous generation's. That is an awful indictment of the rest of us. To paraphrase the great German theologian Reinhold Niebuhr, the mark of any generation is what it leaves for the next one.

By that profoundly important standard, we Boomers have failed you Millennials.

We must all do better.

And we can.

CHAPTER 3

Broken Promises—
the Continuing Litany of Government Failure

Politicians—not statesmen—dominate our public life; there's a big difference. The deficiencies of our elected officials explain in part big government's big failure: this generation will, for the first time, live less well than their parents. But there's much more to it. Where is Milton Friedman now that we really need him?

What we have here is a classic case of dumbass.

—Donald Imus, *Imus in the Morning*

How did we get here? What lies were we told? What promises were made and broken? Looking at history, not as a liberal or conservative, Democrat or Republican, Boomer or Millennial, what can we learn about what *really* works—that is, what improves economic growth, furthers social justice, and expands opportunity for all?

The cumulative evidence clearly suggests that the interplay of millions of people making their own decisions is consistently much more effective than a few government bureaucrats, elected or not, deciding what is in the best interest of the rest of us. Further, the record clearly shows their decisions often have profoundly unintended consequences—all-too-often consequences that are diametrically opposed to the results they were seeking.

So let's start by acknowledging the plain truth, despite countless erstwhile benefits bestowed on Millennials by government—everything from free healthcare for the disadvantaged young to ever-more generous appearing student aid terms—that by virtually any standard, today's Millennials have fallen behind their parents.

If you fall into this age group and are fortunate enough to have gone to college but required financial aid, then you are likely burdened by significant student loan debt.

Furthermore and consequently, few Millennials own their own homes. Your incomes are lower and career tracks less promising. You save less. Your retirement will likely come much later. You will live with more uncertainty about your job security and prospects. But if you're a Millennial, you know this already. You don't need someone writing a book to remind you of that. The notice comes in the mail. E-mail or snail mail, it will find you. And you must pay. These debts cannot be escaped even through bankruptcy.

What you may not realize, because it lies ahead of you, is that your tax burden will be at least twice that of your parents and members of their generation—and quite likely much more. Overall, your standard of living has declined from that of your parents and preceding generations. With the current epidemic of childhood obesity, this generation may even see their expected lifespans decline for the first time in our history!

So, again, how did you—and we—get here? How did what Milton Friedman warned us against actually come to pass?

The Sad End to an Enviable Record

As Friedman noted in 1993, "Since the beginning of our republic, every generation has been better schooled than its predecessor and has had a higher standard of living. The coming generation threatens to be the first for which that is not true, and that would be a major tragedy."

Since then, the Great Recession saw Friedman's prediction and raised it.

The road to this sad place is paved with broken promises. These promises were often made in selfish disregard for the future of our children—you. They were also made in ignorance of—or indifference to—the hard-won economic lessons of history. All this in pursuit of the Baby Boomers' number one conceit—"we can have it all."

We have. Had it all, that is. Until now.

But at our children's expense.

Most important, we have failed to look into the future and see that "same old" won't work anymore. Circumstances have changed. The accumulating burden of ever-expanding entitlement programs, growing government debt, slowing sustainable growth, wasteful and sometimes pitifully-ineffectual government spending, over-regulation and bitter political division—could possibly test the very foundation of our society.

Think Kent State—on a bigger scale.

Like a well-cloaked malignancy that gives few signs of mestasis, you had to know precisely where to look to detect these discouraging circumstances as they crept up on us. Oncologists "stage" cancers, measuring their seriousness by four measures: Stage One (early) to Stage Four (this is where they nicely tell you to get your affairs in order); by this standard, America has missed its chance for early detection ("The best hope for cure"), and is solidly Stage Three—very serious and possibly spreading already throughout the body.

Our country's decline crept up on us like a middle-age weight gain. And all the while, we clung to our familiar assumptions. For example, we Boomers blithely assumed that our children's standard of living would closely resemble our own, especially given their college—and even grad school—educations. Maybe they'd even support us in our old age.

Dream on.

In fact, the Millennials are currently living on the economic edge. To recap some earlier points about employment rates, Millennials of employment age born in the early 1980s and afterward account for 40 percent of the unemployed, or 4.6 million people, and as of June 2014, two million of those have been out of work for at least six months. Your current unemployment rate is 11 percent—or four times that if one counts underemployment in the broadest sense of the term. But having a job isn't everything. There is also net worth—assets (such as savings accounts) minus liabilities (such as student debt). Let's see what's happening there:

- The under-35 crowd has a savings rate of negative 2 percent—the lowest in history, according to Moody's Analytics.
- Two-thirds of recent college graduates have unpaid student loans, with average debt of more than $27,000, reports Pew Research.

(Two decades ago, only half of recent grads had such debt, and the average was $15,000.)

So let's talk about that. Even though it is an unpleasant subject which you would most likely prefer to avoid. But you can't. Those notices come every month.

Debt makes a difference. College-educated adults without student debt have an average net worth of $64,700—about enough to put bread on the table for a year of unemployment. But if they are still paying off school loans, they have only one-fifth that amount, at $8,700. Unless Mom and Dad can help (not a given, considering how long we Boomers are living and how tired we are of putting our retirement dreams on hold). And, to repeat, how we tend to look out for number one, even if that means shortchanging the generations that come after us.

An Average Education Debt of More Than $27,000

Add up all those educational loans and you get to more than $1.2 trillion, $1 trillion of it owed to the federal government. That's a lot less than mortgage debt, which stands at about $8 trillion, most of the more than $11 trillion owed in total by consumers, but it's still serious money. And if you're looking for the next tinderbox that might set off a reprise of the Great Recession, consider these facts:

- That $27,300 average represents a more than 60 percent increase over the past seven years—that's an average annual rise of nearly 9 percent—a time when credit card and auto debt have actually declined!
- The Federal Reserve Bank of New York reports that only 56 percent of borrowers are making payments. At least one third of these loans are 30 days past due—a lot (at its worst, only 10 percent of mortgage holders were delinquent);
- The default rate on federal school loans is 13 percent—and that's just for the first three years. The $1 trillion-plus amount is a significant fraction of what the federal government itself owes credit markets, and equivalent to the $4 trillion that state and local governments owe to those markets—$3 trillion and $1 trillion, respectively
- Changes to the law prevent graduates from having this debt discharged through a personal bankruptcy filing—like so many big

deadbeat companies can do. Debtor grads are on the hook for it forever, vulnerable to having their wages garnished and their credit compromised. They can petition the government to stop payments for a period, but the interest keeps accumulating.

Of course, if the government were held to the same accounting standards as our debt-ridden kids and the rest of us, they'd be obliged to write off hundreds of billions of these toxic assets. But they have their own rules—as well as the ability to reduce the interest rates they charged to reduce this huge overhang—at least in appearance. But that doesn't make the problem go away.

At some point, it will be necessary to raise taxes—a common refrain when it comes to the unintended consequences of government policies.

Studies show that this student debt has led to higher rates of stress and even increasing suicide rates among young people. But you probably didn't need a study to tell you that.

"People who take out significant college loans score worse on quality-of-life measures, a trend that persists into middle age", the *Wall Street Journal* has reported, citing a poll by Gallup Education and Purdue University:

> "Even 24 years after graduation, students who borrowed more than $25,000 are less likely to enjoy work and are less financially and physically fit than their counterparts who graduated without debt. For more recent college grads, the discrepancy is even more pronounced."

Brandon Busteed, director of Gallup Education, notes that "high debt could undermine people's sense of purpose by prompting them to take jobs that pay more rather than ones they are really interested in."

You were educated with a vague plan of employment where you would report to an office every morning, attend meetings, write reports, travel for conferences, dine out on the expense account and take exciting vacations. You are, instead, clerking on the floor of a big box store at a mall somewhere. And you are thinking, "All that money ... for this?"

WHAT'S *REALLY* THE PROBLEM?

So let's ask the logical questions: Why *is* a college education so expensive? And why did I chain myself to a lifetime of debt to acquire one?

There are several factors at work here. Among them:

- Less government support. State and federal appropriations to state schools (and 80 percent of U.S. college students attend public schools) have declined 26 percent since the early 1990s.
- At the same time, the rising cost of compliance with government regulations (e.g., gender discrimination, campus crime—including sexual violence, increasingly strict NCAA rules, among others) are adding millions to costs.
- Tuition discounting (a form of wealth transfer), where institutions charge the affluent a lot, but then discount tuition bills to a rising number of less-comfortable students and their families.
- I propose another: Say's Law. Jean-Baptiste Say, an 18th century French economist, argued that supply creates its own demand. Some suggest that easier access to debt-financed higher education has impaired institutions' fiscal discipline. Put another way, recall Henry Ford's great achievement—not mass production, as many argue, but installment credit. He invented a way for consumers to buy his then-pricey product *over time*. He made it *easy for the customer to buy*—just as college loans do. Put another way, easy college credit creates a trough at which all the pigs feed—not just the colleges themselves. But at a horrific cost.

A recent analysis by Bloomberg, based on U.S. Bureau of Labor and other statistics, showed that the cost of college education has risen faster than inflation for decades—with the most dramatic rise coming in 2004, exactly the time when many Millennials were claiming their sheepskins and writing their first checks to Sallie Mae.

> "Including room and board, costs average $18,943 for in-state students at public schools and $32,762 for out-of-state residents. At private schools, the bill is $42,419. Those amounts don't include items that aren't directly billed by the school, such as transportation, books and laundry."
>
> —College Board, cited by Bloomberg

Figure 2: Education and Medical Prices Skyrocket
While Import Prices Drop

CPI, Percent Change, 2000 to 2009

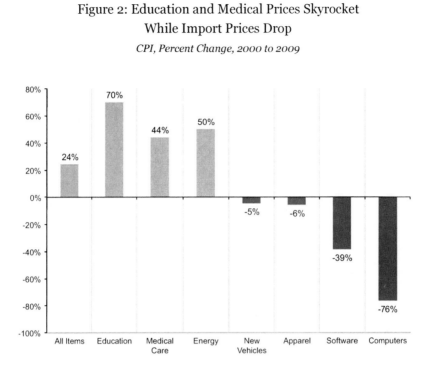

By continually easing access to educational borrowing the government has erected a towering pricing umbrella under which related parties, in addition to the educational institutions themselves, can raise prices. These perverse effects result in rapidly-inflating college costs and, of course, the similarly fast-rising student debt.

Raising those prices and actually charging them can be two different things. In a recent study ("Do the Benefits of College Still Outweigh the Costs"), the Federal Reserve Bank of New York found that "While published tuition and fees represent the 'sticker price' for attending college, many students, if not most, do not actually pay this price"—due to many forms of subsidy. Even after calculating "net tuition cost to reflect this, however, the Fed analysis still noted enormous inflation in the cost of education."

Craig Richardson, professor of economics at Winston-Salem University in North Carolina, described how this shows up in the costs of student textbooks ("The $250 Econ 101 Textbook", *Wall Street Journal*, January 2015)—ironically, Greg Mankiw's *Principles of Economics*, at $350 a copy, it now takes a student "about 35 hours of work after taxes to afford this book. ... I paid about \$20 for a wonderful textbook by Richard Lipsey and Peter Steiner, *Economics* ... minimum wage was \$3.35 then so it took about six hours of work for me to pay for the book."

Figure 3: Annual Published and Net Tuition
for Bachelor's and Associates' Degrees

1970–2013

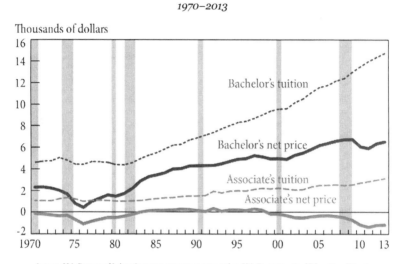

Source: U.S. Bureau of Labor Statistics, consumer price index, U.S. Department of Education, Digest
of Education Statistics 2012: The College Board, Trends in College Pricing 2013 and Trends
in Student Aid 2013.

It isn't just the government. That \$350 helps satisfy teachers' demands for "free examination copies, Power Point decks, lecture notes, quiz generators and so forth"—everything that makes *their* lives easier (but not students'). And let's not forget the annual updates (now electronic and password protected to discourage piracy) which obsolesce the prior year materials, thus killing the used book market and assuring continued (highly profitable—average industry margins surpass 30 percent) full-price demand.

Multiply this across the full spectrum of college costs and we see the problem in full. Elizabeth Warren's "solution" is to ease the burden of borrowing even more—rather than attack the real problem of cost inflation. And in January, 2015 President Obama ignored both problems and recommended free two-year community college!

As Richardson notes, "During the past 30 years, there has been an explosion of student loan debt. Students rarely pay for books out-of-pocket and instead roll it into their financial aid package. So a $250 book is now being paid back over decades ... so here is the $250 text book, a creature of government-subsidized student loans, professors who pay no attention to prices, and students who strive to push the costs down the road."

Is the Parchment Worth It?

You bet. In fact, the implied rate of return on a college degree—about 15 percent—beats the gain on stocks and bonds by a country mile—even for the one-third of college grads who remain "under-employed", i.e., working in jobs that don't require such a degree.

Figure 4: Average Annual Wages, by Education

1970–2013

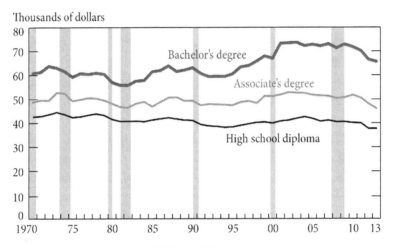

Source: U.S. Census Bureau and U.S Bureau of Labor Statistics, Current Population Survey,
March Supplement, U.S. Bureau of Labor Statistics, cosumer price index.

"Most legislation aimed at eliminating unhappiness and discontent has resulted in misery. ... Government is an organic cultural organism. It lives by growing and it lives by accretion. It will arrogate to itself all the power it can by the apparent mech-anism of legislation and the less apparent but more virulent op-eration of bureaucratic growth, by usage, and precedent. ... The Liberal state, in the worthy desire to exorcise greed, poverty, and unhappiness, has given birth to a radical view of the world: that it is the responsibility of the State to protect anyone who may claim to be powerless. But what check is upon these champions? And what inducement do they possess to refrain, since to refrain is to diminish their power? And, so, their livelihoods? Is it not evident that to be accused before the bureaucrats of OSHA, Equal Employment Opportunity Commission, FDA, Consumer Safety Board, and so on, is to be found guilty, for the organization's first and only responsibility is to grow, and, in contrast to the free market, it is not the populace, but the government which characterizes failure and success, and that all government programs must not only expand after success, but expand after failure, in order "to bring about eventual success." Note that all this hocus-pocus is taking place with the money actually earned by hardworking individuals."

—David Mamet, *The Secret Knowledge*

The current Washington administration of some 80,000 federal check-collectors "work" for an individual who was elected on a plank that decreed that wealth be redistributed so to narrow the widening income gap between rich and the poor. We see this redistributionist theme in Obamacare for sure, but also in tuition discounting, as well as in the increasingly progressive tax code, in the unprecedented boost to the minimum wage and extension of unemployment benefits for 24 months, and perhaps most dramatic of all, the growth in food stamp (Supplemental Nutrition Assistance Program) recipients from 17 million in 1980 to 48 million in 2013—with much of the increase occurring in the past few years during a supposed economic recovery.

But where we see it most glaringly—and tacitly—is in the enormous burden that has been placed implicitly on the young to provide for Boomer needs and the needs of the elderly. As Pete Peterson notes in *Running On Empty*, "young people, according to official Social Security trustees' numbers, are *already expected* to pay the equivalent of 25 to 40 percent of their payroll into Social Security and Medicare before they retire just to keep these programs solvent."

Figure 5: Monthly Food Stamp Participation

April 2007–June 2013 (in millions)

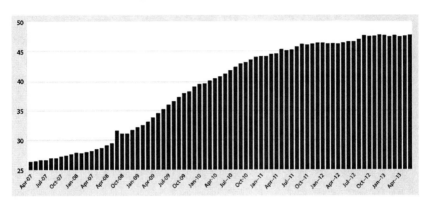

Source: Wall Street's Brightest Minds Reveal the Most Important Charts in the World,
Wall Street Journal.

Nowhere is this clearer than in government's intrusion in the health-care industry. As mentioned, in 2013 total government spending on the two programs was about $1 trillion. Just imagine how much lower that would be if those clever managers in Washington could curtail fraud.

But, hey, this is the government. Where is the incentive?

> "If a private enterprise is a failure, it closes down—unless it can get a government subsidy to keep it going; if a government enterprise fails, it is expanded. … The general rule is that government undertakes an activity that seems desirable at the time. Once the activity begins, whether it proves desirable or not, people in both the government and the private sector acquire a vested interest in it. If the initial reason for undertaking the activity disappears, they have a strong incentive to find another justification for its continued existence."
>
> —Milton Friedman, *Why Government is the Problem*

Where next can we find government failure? Golly, where to start?

- What of farm subsidies where we pay farmers to support them, whether they grow crops or not (in more than one out of five cases they are in effect paid not to grow the crops)? That costs $5 billion a year.

- Or tariffs of one kind or another—for example, our quota on imported sugar, which drives up its cost (but benefited the Fanjol family, major sugar growers in Florida who were ubiquitous political contributors, including to Vermont junior Senator and champion of campaign finance reform, Bernie Sanders).
- Or our failing infrastructure?
- Or housing?

CAN THE GOVERNMENT RUN ANYTHING?

Apologists for the present system will say that today's divided and divisive Congress precludes any kind of useful collaboration. We say "nonsense."

Look at the Veterans' Administration. There is no significant political opposition to its mission and no one opposes spending "whatever it takes" to take care of those who sacrificed for their country.

But look at government's record.

> "Intelligent people may look at the excess of big corporations and be appalled by the lack of connection between the will of the shareholders and the operations of the business. They may be shocked by the out of control executive compensation. Why, they may ask, do the shareholders not take the control which is theirs? But these questioners, on the Left, will not ask the same question of that largest and most bloated of all corporations, the American Government. And well they might."
>
> —David Mamet, *The Secret Knowledge*

PART TWO

How We Got Here

CHAPTER 4

Predictably, You Voted for Them!

Just because the government doesn't think clearly is no reason for us not to. Millennials can change the path of America, and Boomers can help, but we all better get smart fast. At the very least, we must hold the government to much higher standards, and we must elevate the debate on public policies—especially in the coming election. And Millennials can help bridge the partisan gap—and maybe encourage the right wing of the GOP to embrace (or at least to tolerate) others' values on social issues.

So tell me who I see
When I look in your eyes
Is that you baby
Or just a brilliant disguise.

—Bruce Springsteen, "Brilliant Disguise"

I t's axiomatic that we don't like politicians, but we all love our Congressman. They are a seductive crew, these politicians, affable, empathic, often articulate. But are they for real? And, are they competent? Or are they often simply gifted hypocrites?

It's so hard to know.

And it's hard to know because the trustworthy analysis we need to properly evaluate them and their performance is so hard to come by.

Economists have a couple of terms for such predicaments: "information asymmetry" and "search costs". The first refers to the disparity or congruence of information, the second to how much effort and expense is needed to get to it. Typically, information sets relating to politicians (e.g., how a politician describes his performance vs. how knowledgeable and objective analysts might view it) can be quite disparate—sometimes by intent. And search costs are very high—just look at the variance in views expressed by the highly-respected *New York Times* and *Wall Street Journal*. This is all complicated enormously by the arcane rituals associating with writing law—rituals which almost defy a layman's understanding and force us to rely on interpreters, interpreters who all-too-often are biased.

Figure 6: Disparate Information Sets—and High 'Search Costs'

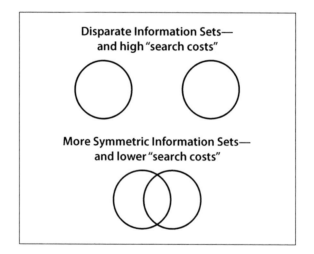

But we've got a terrific thing going for us as we try to parse the truth of public life today—the Internet. Nothing in the history of man has done more to cohere widely disparate information sets and make them more easily accessible to us.

And no one uses the Net more effectively than younger Americans.

Thank God We Can Just 'Google It'

During their lives, Millennials saw iPods reach more than half of U.S. homes in four years, Internet access 10, cell phones 14; by contrast, it took 71 years to get to that penetration rate for telephones and 52 years to get half the country electrified.

The young are used to a world that changes before their eyes while many of us long for a world that never changes at all.

One might argue that you Millennial voters—those most at risk from the rapidly escalating government financial commitments—could very well shift the electoral balance in American politics.

There are 80 million of you—40 percent of the voters.

There's just one problem—you don't vote.

The historical indifference of the young, which has proven so costly to you, may be changing.

While in 2012, the "key to President Obama's solid Electoral College victory was his advantage among the growing population of nonwhite voters," reported the *National Journal*, a magazine for campaign consultants and others, "Millennials ticked up from 12 percent of the electorate in 2008 to 19 percent (in 2012) and once again provided Obama an overwhelming (if slightly reduced from four years ago) three-fifths of their votes."

"Each of the key groups in Obama's coalition of the ascendant is growing in society," the *Journal* said. Morley Winograd, with the Democratic advocacy group NDN and coauthor of two books on the Millennial, predicts, "We think this coalition (of minorities, young and just enough college-educated whites) is not only ascendant but will be dominant."

The Democratic organization Campaign for America chortles about the other constituent parts of this ascendant block that went big for Obama: women (51 percent of the vote, 67 percent to Obama), African Americans (13 percent of the vote; 93 percent for Obama), Latinos (10 percent of the electorate, 75 percent for Obama), LGBT (5 percent, but 77 percent for the President), and Asian Americans (just 3 percent, but 73 percent for Obama).

Just how sound is the Left's optimism?

Not far off the mark. The GOP has a lot of work to do if it's going to restore some balance to our politics.

Nixon's 'Enemies List' and Yours

In the early Seventies, I worked for the CEO of a Fortune 100 company. He counted many achievements in his long career, including the exploit—during his Air Force service—of being part of the first flight crew to fly over the North Pole. Among his proudest accomplishments, though, was his unique appearance twice on Nixon's enemies list. He kept the relevant page of the Congressional Record framed on the wall of the private rest room in his opulent office.

The purpose of the list was revealed by White House counsel John Dean during the Watergate hearings in 1972, when he characterized a memo on "Dealing with Our Political Enemies" as addressing "how we can maximize the fact of our incumbency in dealing with persons known to be active in their opposition to our Administration; stated a bit more bluntly—how we can use the available federal machinery to screw our political enemies."

Of course, we all look askance at this particular enemies list but is the concept really so bad?

Millennials might even consider composing a similar "enemies list" of special interest groups fighting to preserve and enrich the unwieldy entitlement programs for which they will get the bill.

They might well begin with the organizations listed in *Running on Empty*:
- AARP, 37 million members (the Millennials' No. 1 enemy)
- Retired Public Employees Association, 40,000 members
- Military Officers Association of America (formerly, The Retired Officers Association), 380,000 members
- American Medical Association, 250,000 members
- American Hospital Association, 5,000 hospitals and 40,000 individuals
- American Legion, 2.4 million members
- AMVETS, 250,000 members
- Pork and cotton lobbies
- Medical equipment and nursing home lobbies
- Ethanol and peanut lobbies
- Century Fund
- Economic Policy Institute
- National Association of Social Insurance
- Families USA
- National Committee to Preserve Social Security and Medicare.

When they vote, the young have historically voted liberal. A 2014 poll by the Reason Foundation, a Libertarian organization, found that

43 percent of the young see themselves as Democrats compared to just 23 percent who identify as Republicans. 53 percent said they'd support Hillary Clinton for President in 2016—three times more than would support Rand Paul, their favorite non-Democratic candidate. In the last election, they went big for Obama because, Anna Bliss argued in Mic.com, "they could not distinguish between Romney and Obama on fiscal policy, thus, they voted on social issues"—namely, the "as long as it doesn't hurt anyone else" attitude toward gay marriage, gay rights, minimum/living wage rules, legalized marijuana, and immigration. But there are signs of balance here. They rightly see the GOP, the party of Lincoln, favorably on issues of racial justice. And a recent Pew report showed that Millennials are not so gung-ho on abortion-on-demand and environmental regulations as some liberals might wish. So given that today the GOP needs to win in a few big states, like Texas and Georgia, to just have a chance in a national election, the young offer the best hope for restoring some competitive balance to American political life.

Pew Research also confirms that Republican Millennials are just as fervent in their views about social issues as their more liberal brethren—implying that Republicans can appeal to them by emphasizing economic issues and replacing the talk of social issues with a legitimate concern about individual freedom that goes to the heart and history of the GOP.

Millennials can take up some other issues that promise to restore promise to our future—things like term limits. Mark Twain put the case for term limits well when he observed that "politicians and diapers should be changed frequently—and for the same reason."

CHAPTER 5

'May I Have the Bill, Please?'

The New World of Hobson's choice—higher taxes ... or higher taxes? The debt is huge and still growing. Millennials get this huge bill—which, by one measure, amounts to almost $700,000 for every man, woman and child in the U.S.! Is the tipping point near?

If a country has not balanced its long-run budget when the long-run arrives, then the market balances its budget for it—and does so in a way that nobody likes. ... (T)he long-run seems to vary between three years and 200, depending.

—Brad DeLong, Berkeley economics professor and former Clinton advisor

Sitting at the Oak Bar in New York's Plaza Hotel many years ago, a friend who worked for now-defunct Continental Illinois Bank as a lending officer explained how the loan he'd just made would benefit the bank's earnings per share by five cents in the next quarter. I was impressed. After all, we were mere plebes in the financial world—just getting started. And the Oak Bar was a great place for a grandiose discussion.

Wishing to fully appreciate my friend's accomplishment, I arrayed the many cocktail napkins he'd used in his calculations in their correct order and studied them carefully.

"Congratulations. You're math is great. There's just one problem."

"Oh, yeah," he said, looking up from the dry Rob Roy on the rocks, "What's that?"

"You misplaced couple of decimal points," I replied.

So, too, it is in looking at government numbers. They are so BIG as to be beyond our imagination. So big, in fact, that you wonder whether the folks putting them out are lying to us—fearful perhaps, as Jack Nicholson might say, that we "can't stand the truth!"

Brace yourself. This is like the part of the physical exam where you are asked to bend over and flex your knees (or place your feet in the stirrups).

There's no way to put lipstick on this pig. There are 321 million people in the U.S. and apparently the only ones who can't count are in a place called Washington, D.C. They've been telling us one thing for years—most recently, that federal government debt is more than $13 trillion—when the truth was far, far different. The way they justified that was by developing their own accounting—sort of like Bernie Madoff and that nice Italian guy from Boston named Ponzi.

Reality is very different.

$700,000 Owed by Every Man, Woman and Child!

The "fiscal gap" is far more meaningful. This concept was developed by Laurence Kotlikoff and his colleagues; it starts with the CBO's most realistic long-term budget forecast, assumes that earlier-mentioned debt in the hands of the public ($10 trillion), assumes non-interest and spending growth of 2 percent a year, discounts the difference between noninterest spending and taxes, then discounts that (at a 3 percent rate). That gets us to a fiscal gap of $212 trillion—many times the number you keep hearing about. That's almost $700,000 for every man, woman, and child in the country!

The second idea, for which Kotlikoff and crew again deserve our thanks, is "generational accounting", a fresh concept that seeks to measure how much it will cost our children to close this fiscal gap—either through higher taxes, lower government spending or some combination of the two.

Is either of these concepts perfect? Of course not.

But they attempt to be honest—and that's a refreshing change. You will not hear these concepts from our elected officials. They are too scary, and voters don't like scary.

According to the CBO, to close our fiscal gap could take a permanent 64 percent boost to all federal taxes, or a 40 percent cut in spending!

Hard to imagine how either will happen. But, with an overhang like this staring Millennials in the face, at least your attention will be heightened the next time a politician extends a bribe—say, for student loan relief.

FEDERAL BUDGET SIMPLIFIED

At the very top line, and this necessarily over-simplifies a very complex and political subject, the give/get of the federal budget isn't THAT complicated. NOTE—In 2012, the Federal government raised $2.3 trillion and borrowed an additional $1.1 trillion. Bear in mind, importantly, that state and local taxes add 58 cents for every dollar that Washington collects.

WHERE DOES ALL THAT MONEY GO?

Figure 7: Federal Budget Expenditures by Category

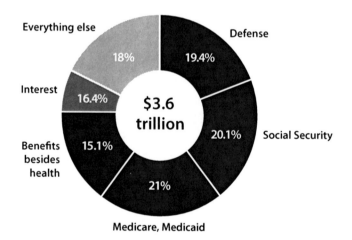

Many observers are struck by how misinformed the American public is about government spending. As David Wessel notes in his book *Red Ink: Inside The High Stakes Of The Federal Budget* (Crown Press, 2012), "a 2008 Cornell University poll in which 44 percent of those who receive Social Security checks and 40 percent of those covered by Medicare say that 'have not used a government social program.'"

The chart above shows where our taxes go. What doesn't show here, however, is the part that gets all the attention—the part of federal spending that gets allocated annually—and this amounts to less than a fifth of total outlays. The big part is mandatory spending—interest (more about this in a few pages), Social Security and the healthcare programs.

And Where Does All the Money Come From?

Figure 8: The Changing Tax Mix

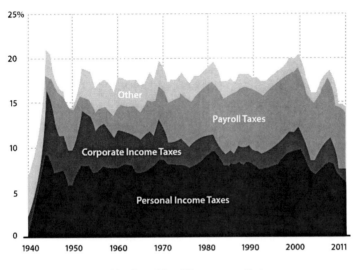

Source: White House Office of Management and Budget

It comes from borrowing ... and from us! And it comes two ways—personal income taxes, and payroll taxes on us and our employers. By contrast, the tax on corporate profits is a much smaller source of tax revenue—and a declining one. Here, let's be cautious for this is quick sand politically—as the frequent cries of populists make clear.

In fact, corporations do conduct themselves so that they minimize their taxes—just as we do. This is one reason so many of them pay no corporate taxes!

But There's a Second Source of Revenue
for the Government—Borrowing.

U.S. GDP is $17.6 trillion. All government debt in the credit markets—state, local, federal—adds up to $4 trillion, as mentioned earlier. Off balance sheet debt is even higher—$5 trillion for guarantees on mortgage-backed securities alone, note Harvard researchers in an April 2014 study of Fiscal Risk and the Portfolio of Government Programs. The federal government typically starts the fiscal year without a budget, but if they had one it would be about $3 trillion today, and we would expect them to post a deficit of more than $500 billion. (This omits the value of future obligations.)

Let's look again at today's average interest rate on Federal debt—2.38 percent—relative to the $13 trillion in debt outstanding. We're running an interest tab of more than $300 billion. Now flash forward—let's move the interest rate on that debt to the average rate of the past decade or about 5 percent. Under this scenario, we would pay nearly twice as much interest on the debt. How does a $600 billion interest tab sound to you?

Of course, public debt doesn't really tell us much about the gravity of our plight. It's only when you properly account for our future obligations and get up to that $211 trillion number that picture clarifies.

So Far, So Good—But for How Long?

Observers, government officials especially, assume that it's our problem to work out—but the lesson of history teaches us the world—and markets—don't work that way. They occasionally cry "Enough!" and riot.

So, two questions arise: who owns the U.S. debt and long will they tolerate our financial irresponsibility?

Foreigners own more than a third of the debt—and this includes China (7.2 percent), and some "bad boy" countries like Venezuela, Iran, Iraq, and Libya (about 3 percent). Does such ownership confer influence? Perhaps at some point. Selling such debt suddenly could obviously have disastrous effect on interest rates and the U.S. interest bill. For the time being, we may console ourselves with the rhetorical question, "What rational person yells 'Fire!' in a crowded theater?" But simply turning to another currency—i.e., putting their excess savings into some other country's bonds—could wreak calamity as well.

Again we return to the issue of GDP and our nation's productivity, and thus our ability to pay what we owe. Here's what the Congressional Budget Office has to show and tell on the matter.

"Federal spending would increase to 26 percent of GDP by 2039 under the assumptions of the extended baseline, CBO projects, compared with 21 percent in 2013 and an average of 20.5 percent over the past 40 years.

"Federal revenues would also increase relative to GDP under current law, but much more slowly than federal spending.

"The gap between federal spending and revenues would widen after 2015 under the assumptions of the extended baseline. ... Moreover, the harmful effects that such large debt would have on the economy would worsen the budget outlook. Under current law, the increase in debt relative to the size of the economy, combined with a gradual increase in marginal tax rates (the rates that would apply to an additional dollar of income), would reduce economic output and raise interest rates, compared with the benchmark economic projections that CBO used in producing the extended baseline. Those economic effects in turn would lead to lower federal revenues and higher interest payments on the debt. With those effects included, federal debt held by the public under the extended baseline would rise to 111 percent of GDP in 2039."

—Sources: CBO, July and December 2014.

Bad though this picture is, it gets worse.

We must now add the cost of the entitlement programs, largely driven by folks like me—the aging-of-America segment (or cohort, as the demographers say) who get Social Security and who make increasing use of rapidly-inflating healthcare services via Medicare and Medicaid.

A Gordian Knot of Public Policy Choices—All Bad

So there's the problem in a nutshell. Pay close attention. A huge debt, which grows remorselessly and rapidly, driven by rising entitlement spending for an aging population (which—unlike you Millennials—votes in large numbers and thus defends its entitlements) and a very limited margin of spending over which public officials can actually exercise any influence in the short-run.

As bad as it is, it gets worse.

Until the recent Great Recession, a pattern repeated itself over many decades, both here and abroad—call it a negative paradigm or feedback loop. The inevitable downturns in the economy were then followed by government and central bank efforts to induce a recovery by lowering interest rates and/or deficit spending until GDP revived, with any distress tempered by a growing host of post-Depression palliatives like unemployment and deposit insurance, food stamps, and the like. The unfortunate consequence? Excesses never got completely wrung out of the system; instead, they accumulated as debt. Over time, like a magnificent old tree with rot at its center, this has created a very wobbly economic structure with ever-declining and increasingly fragile liquidity at its heart. And even today's zero interest rates have proved insufficient to induce consumer spending or bank lending—so the government has done so through Quantitative Easing and assumed the debt in place of the private sector!

And so the ratio of debt to GDP continues to rise around the world and will likely continue to do so until growth resumes at a robust rate.

But when and where can we look for that?

Some would say, we can inflate our way out, but how are we going to fool the markets, which will inevitably demand higher interest rates to compensate for depreciating principal values? And, besides, most of the world is suffering from—or on the brink of—deflation, not inflation. Indeed, the only way to support today's high debt levels is via continued very low interest rates.

Will Japan's fate prove to be our own? Or Europe's?

In a recent report, "Debt and (not much) deleveraging", from the McKinsey Global Institute, the authors suggest that we are in uncharted waters:

> "It is clear that deleveraging is rare and that solutions are in short supply. Given the scale of debt in the most highly indebted countries, the current solutions for sparking growth or cutting fiscal deficits will not be sufficient. New approaches are needed to start deleveraging and to manage and monitor debt. This includes innovations in mortgages and other debt contracts to better share risk; clearer rules for restructuring debt; eliminating

tax incentives for debt; and using macroprudential measures to dampen credit booms. Debt remains an essential tool for funding economic growth. But how debt is created, used, monitored and when needed discharged, must be improved."

The hallmark of great tragedy is its growing sense of inevitability. Get the picture?

Remember that mime we Boomers did for our kids?

" You must pay the rent!"

"But I can't pay the rent!"

Enter the hero. "Well, I'll pay the rent"

Fair maiden, sighing with relief: "My hero."

Well, this is the real world. The rent must be paid.

And guess who gets to pay it?

That's right, Ms. Millennial—you do.

So far, our focus has been on federal debt woes. The picture doesn't get any better at the state or local level. Just look at California where the Terminator himself met his match. As Michael Lewis points out in his breezy, but insightful tour of the third world (i.e., Greece, Iceland) debt debacle, Schartzeneger had "come to power in the bust after the Internet bubble; he'd left in the bust after the housing bubble." We don't think of Arnold as a loser, but in California trying to apply simple common sense to the State's intractable financial problems (which got worse after he left office), he lost big.

> "In November 2005 he called a special election that sought votes on four reforms: limiting state spending, putting an end to the gerrymandering of legislative districts, limiting public employee union spending on elections, and lengthening the time it took for public school teachers to get tenure. All four propositions addressed, directly or indirectly, the state's large and growing mess. All four were defeated; the votes weren't even close."
>
> —Michael Lewis, *Boomerang*, 2011

Unable to fix the state, the problems were pushed to local communities where the same high compensation and rich retirement packages for public sector employees doomed them to service cutbacks and, in increasing cases, bankruptcy. Just as they did in Detroit and other failed cities across America.

Lewis asks, why?

He gets one answer from UCLA's Dr. Peter Whybrow, who argues in *American Mania* that it's our fault—our brains, trained to focus on what is scarce (e.g., sex, food, safety), try to get as much of them as possible. Despite our present abundance, those brains, with their reptilian centers dominating, can no longer temper their acquisitive hunger.

The succession of financial bubbles and the amassing of personal and public debt, Whybrow views as simply an expression of the lizard-brain way of life. A color-coded map of American personal indebtedness could be laid on top of the Centers for Disease Control's color-coded map that illustrates the fantastic rise in rates of obesity across the United States since 1985 without disturbing the general pattern. The boom in day-trading activity in individual stock portfolios; the spread of legalized gambling; the rise of drug and alcohol addiction; it is all of a piece. Everywhere you turn, you see Americans sacrifice their long-term interests for a short-term reward.

I offer another answer: officials caving in to public sector union wage demands and, via extravagantly generous retirement concessions that come due later, kicking the can down the road (past the next election).

As daunting as the rapidly growing IOU run up by our officials may be, even more astonishing is the way they attempt to fund their out-of-control spending.

Perhaps no one has chronicled this lunacy better than Arthur Laffer, who conceived the Laffer Curve.

Popularized during the Reagan administration, the curve shows the tradeoff between tax rates and tax revenues.

Today's "tax the rich" redistributionists struggle to accept this idea that by lowering tax rates, governments can increase tax revenues—often by quite a bit. At the same time, tax cuts stimulate growth, multiplying employment and opportunity. Though seldom acknowledged, this is a truly bipartisan concept. One of our youngest and most charismatic presidents—a Democrat—understood these concepts very well and was the first to implement them.

Figure 9: The Laffer Curve

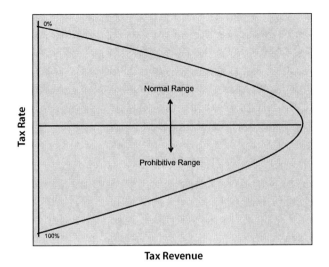

Tax Revenue

When John Kennedy campaigned for president in 1960, he pledged to "get the country moving again." Once in office, he wasted no time in reintroducing the American people to two economic concepts that would comprise the fulcrum of his effort: "fiscal drag" and the "full employment budget surplus"—both drawn from the work of British economist John Maynard Keynes (who demonstrated his well-known conviviality by replying on his death bed to the question: "Do you have any regrets?" with, "Just one. I wish I'd had more champagne.").

The first concept was the extent to which the economy was hurt as rising incomes in a progressive tax system pushed wage-earners into higher tax brackets; the latter was a related estimate of what government deficit or surplus would be if the economy was performing well. To nudge the economy there, Kennedy proposed—and Congress enacted in 1965—massive tax cuts, cutting the top marginal rate from 91 percent to 70 percent (still well above today's rate). In the years following, government tax revenue increased—at an increasing rate! The reason is simple. The supplier of tax revenues did incrementally better—hence the term "supply side" economics.

In his 1963 Economic Report of the President, Kennedy had this to say:

"Yet many taxpayers seemed prepared to deny the nation the fruits of tax reduction because they question the financial soundness of reducing taxes when the federal budget is already in deficit. Let me make clear why, in today's economy, fiscal prudence and responsibility call for tax reduction even if it temporarily enlarged the federal deficit—why reducing taxes is the best way open to us to increase revenues."

He was seconded on the House Floor by Ways and Means chairman (and Democrat) Wilbur Mills:

"Mr. Chairman, there is no doubt in my mind that this tax reduction bill, in and of itself, can bring about an increase in the gross national product of approximately $50 billion in the next few years. If it does, these lower rates of taxation will bring in at least $12 billion in additional revenue."

It's worth noting, as do Laffer and *Return to Prosperity* co-author Stephen Moore, that years later Kennedy's chairman of the Council of Economic Advisors, Walter Heller, acknowledged the effort's good result before Congress in 1975:

"What happened to the tax cut in 1965 is difficult to pin down, but insofar as we are able to isolate it, it did seem to have a tremendously stimulative effect, a multiplied effect on the economy. It was the major factor that led to our running a $3 billion surplus by the middle of 1965 before escalation in Vietnam struck us. It was a $12 billion tax cut, which would be about $33 or $34 billion in today's terms, and within one year the revenues into the Federal Treasury were already above what they had been before the tax cut.
"Did the tax cut pay for itself in increased revenues? I think the evidence is very strong that it did."

Sixteen years later, Reagan did the same thing, dropping the top marginal rate from that 70 percent to 50 percent. Again, government revenue rose immediately. Reagan didn't stop: in fact, he dropped all the rates by 25 percent over a three-year period.

As Laffer and Moore note, "The most controversial portion of Reagan's tax revolution was the big drop in the highest marginal income rate from 70 percent when he took office to 28 percent in 1988. However, Internal Revenue service data reveal that tax collections from the wealthy, as measured by personal income taxes paid by top-percentile earners, increased between 1980 and 1988 despite significantly lower rates."

> "19th Century British parliamentarian Lord Brougham borrowed from Virgil's description of the monster Fuma to describe the recent invention of the income tax: 'At first small from timidity, but soon rising to giant size, her feet on the earth but her head in the clouds.' So it soon proved."

CUTTING THE ENORMOUS COST OF TAX COMPLIANCE

If people with different political views can't agree on supply side approaches as basic as that described above—an approach embraced by both Kennedy and Reagan—perhaps we can concur on the sheer overwhelming complexity of our tax code and the enormous cost imposed on us for compliance with it. At last count, the Code contained some four million words and took up 70,000 printed pages. But the code is only one small part of the puzzle. There are also the forms that taxpayers must fill out. According to flat tax advocate Robert E. Hall, the IRS sends out eight billion forms per year to 100 million taxpayers. "Placed end to end," says Hall, "these pages would stretch 694,000 miles, or 28 times around the earth." Put Federal, state, and local taxes together and they add up to some $6 trillion—nearly one-third of our $17.4 trillion GDP. The cost to collect this revenue is enormous. The IRS itself admits that it is a "multibillion dollar industry"—and Laffer and Moore put the toll as high as $65 billion.

Even with all that, professional tax advisors usually get it wrong. *Money* magazine hires several firms to complete the same family's return each year. They all typically reach a different conclusion about the amount owed. *USA Today* does a similar test, with the same result. Laffer and Moore note that tax-preparation cost is "only part of the actual costs paid by taxpayers in terms of time spent and personal costs that have not been outsourced. ... To be precise, the IRS Taxpayer Advocate calculates that individuals and businesses spend 7.6 billion hours a year complying with the U.S. tax code ... (or) $193 billion ..."

The two authors also quote the Tax Foundation's compliance estimate ($265 billion for 2006), projected to increase to almost $500 billion in 2015.

Not only is "the bill" big and growing, but it is devilishly hard—and expensive—to actually compute.

Let's Try Something New

Though tax experts dispute its practicality in today's adversarial political climate, a flat tax, like that championed by Steve Forbes during his presidential bids, would solve many of these issues. Do away with things like oil depletion, accelerated depreciation, and countless others—make it all simple with a national sales tax. Try it and watch the special interests come out, though. And guess what—we all have "special interests"—you and I don't want to see the deductibility of home interest go away, do we? Or, say, charitable deductions?

And soon we will realize that all that complexity arises from an effort to be "fair" (there's that word again); after all, the insurance industry isn't like the car manufacturing business, so the tax code must reflect the differences to be "fair."

You can see the challenge. It won't be easy.

Meanwhile, some are trying other ways to minimize the tax burden— like, for example, barter.

Recent decades have seen the emergence of retail barter exchanges, corporate barter companies, and complementary currency organizations, in Argentina and elsewhere—all engaging in transactions without the use of cash. One sign of their existence is the emergence of an International Reciprocal Trade Association, which claims to have helped 40,000 businesses to move some $12 billion in value Excess Business Capacities and underperforming assets in 2014 alone. Those who barter may have been motivated by a desire to save on their taxes, but alas, the tax man still cometh. In Argentina, the tax officials are still trying to keep one step ahead of their people, with a new tax on barters involving stock; and in the U.S., the Internal Revenue Service has a whole set of rules for the taxation of barter-based value as income.

CHAPTER 6

'Sorry, We're in No Position to Help You.'

Boomers may think they've benefitted from this financial irre-sponsibility, but we will get clipped, too. Some say the "perfect generational storm" is upon us, but we will all pay the price. You want to change the world, Millennial? Be our guest.

"The reality is that each postwar administration, starting with Eisenhower, picked the pockets of children to benefit current tax-payers. Moreover, even when taxes were raised to pay for spending, the young generally got to pay the taxes and the elderly generally got to enjoy the spending."

—Kotlikoff and Burns, *The Coming Generational Storm*

O ver half a century, rising home ownership became the hall-mark of America's growing middle class. The number of new single family homes grew rapidly and continually, marked indelibly by communities like Long Island's Levittown—great places with safe neighborhoods where kids, Millennials among them, grew up with personal bedrooms, a lawn big enough for backyard basketball and big barbecues—all of it within reach of a good school system that provided a further stepping stone for the most talented among them.

That's changing today.

Today's Baby Boomers, when they go looking in the deceased parent's safe deposit box, may find unpaid mortgages there. Instead of visiting their local bank to deposit Dad's CDs, they may discover bankers waiting for someone to make up the mortgage delinquency.

Just as Millennials are increasingly foreclosed from buying a home, Baby Boomers appear destined to go to their graves with an outstanding mortgage.

This is a big change for all of us. But it's one of many as Boomers' financial distress converges with that of our kids.

Prior generations celebrated their last house payment with "mortgage burnings"; no more. The same housing bubble that led to the Great Recession led also to the Boomers refinancing their homes, sometimes to buy second homes, often bought with smaller down payments, or other spending. Still more tapped mortgage-based equity lines of credit like an ATM.

Chastened, millions look into the future and worry what rising interest rates will do to their monthly bills. (For some, their employment prospects impaired, that future appears grave indeed. Labor Department data show that joblessness for adults 65 years and older was almost 18 weeks recently, versus 13.5 for those 25 to 34.)

Donald Fromeyer, president of the National Association of Mortgage Brokers, speculates that Baby Boomers don't "have the same desire to pay it off as the generation that went through WWII." Maybe so, but the reality of bigger mortgage borrowing later in life seems so strongly fixed, whether by circumstance or preference, it's unlikely to be altered as Millennials delay buying homes.

And don't underestimate the threat of rising interest rates. Many economists would say that today's average 30-year fixed mortgage rate of well under 4 percent is underpriced owing to Federal Reserve efforts to suppress short-term interest rates in order to thereby spark economic recovery. Re-priced to an historic average of more than 8 percent (the average for the Baby Boomer generation), that means that the monthly interest payment on the average mortgage would easily double. So for those with an interest-only mortgage (as many are) that means twice the price. Absent ceilings in the mortgage contract, a $2,000 mortgage payment will become a $4,000 mortgage payment. Flash forward to a period when the inflation rate nudges upward from today's under-2 percent (for a 10-year

Treasury)—say toward the post-WW II average of 3.78 percent—and the dollars used to pay that mortgage will start losing value, increasing the tab. And don't forget, today's retiring Boomers lived through the '70s, when the prime rate—the rate that big banks charge their most credit-worthy customers—hit 22 percent!

Another problem that will plague both Millennials and Baby Boomers when interest rates return to normal levels will be educational debt. That's right, it isn't just a problem for the young. Earlier in this book we talked about the heavy student debt load that Millennials bear. But their parents bear it, too. According to the Federal Reserve Bank of New York, 6.9 million Americans 50 or older had student loans in 2012, more than doubling from three million in 2005. About 155,000—most of them disability income recipients—had their Social Security checks cut last year after defaulting on their student loans. Older Americans in fact have the highest default rates—more than half of the 260,000 loans to 75 and older folks were in default in 2013—versus a default rate of 12 percent for those 25–49. And these loans weren't taken out to fund their kids' education; *they were taken out for their own.*

Are you getting the picture? The fancy word is "intergenerational altruism" and it's in decline as Aging Boomers and their parents consume more. Maybe it's the flipside of the "narcissistic altruism" we earlier attributed to the Vermont hippies. But the message is the same—when it comes to having the financial resources to help our kids, *we don't have it.*

The New 'Golden Oldie'—Die Broke

Millennials, looking to their parents for help with educational debt or that first mortgage, must increasingly look elsewhere. "Die broke" is the new anthem of the seniors. You see it in their "spend rate"—how much of their wealth they use in a given year. In 1960, it was 9 percent; today it's 14 percent. And life spans are growing each year! Sorry, but it's unlikely there will be much left for you, Junior.

You see it, too, in the growing popularity of "spend-down" reverse mortgages, where we extract built-up equity in our home over time. Such mortgages jumped dramatically at the beginning of the Great Recession and remain at a high level today.

Boomers are also taking many steps to get cash out of their life insurance policies—ranging from a simple borrowing against the value of a whole life policy to a viatical settlement, where a person deemed to be close to death (due to illness or extreme age) exchanges paid-up life insurance for an immediate lump sum lower than the net survivor benefit.

In the case of life insurance cash-outs, there is an entire industry there to do it, and even an association, called the Life Insurance Settlement Association, which recently reported (citing The Deal Pipeline) that transactions in the secondary market grew to $2.57 billion in face value of policies sold in 2013, compared to $2.12 billion in 2012.

And don't look to your maiden aunt for help. Dear old Sadie, a fixture at holidays and a loving presence always, is in no position to help. If she is like her cohorts, she earns far less than your married mom: In 2012, never-married women earned $594 per week, compared to $751 earned by full-time working married women, reports Catalyst.

Don't Get Sore

We Boomers were lied to as well. And the promises made to us—of a secure retirement via Social Security and access to healthcare via Medicare—are in serious jeopardy—at the same time that the Great Recession has reduced our net worth and eroded our employment prospects, never good when you pass 50.

What we have is a perfect demographic storm. And the reason is pretty simple: as we have emphasized throughout these pages and Kotlikoff and Burns point out in *The Coming Generational Storm*, "Basically, all the forces that can enlarge the retired elderly population are in overdrive. The forces that would expand the younger (and working) population paying Social Security and Medicare taxes are in reverse."

And when you slice and dice that 2030 population, you will be surprised to discover that the fastest-growing segment will be the 85-plus crew! As Kotlikoff and Burns note, "In 1960 most of the dependents were children. In the future, most of the dependents will be adults." Baby Boomers are going from changing diapers to wearing them.

Age Dependency Ratios for the United States Based on the Most Recent U.S. Census

"Most countries, including the U.S., are projected to see the share of their population that is 65 and older surpass the share that is younger than 15 by mid-century. Africa's population is projected to increase the most and make up a greater share of the global population by 2050. The shares of Europe and Asia in the global population are expected to decrease, while the Americas will hold steady."

—Pew Research

Declining birth and fertility rates throughout the West don't hold a stick to the challenge facing Mother Russia, where, say Kotlikoff and Burns, "the population could fall from its present 148 million to only 58 million in 2040—a decline of 60 percent! That's comparable to what happened during the plague years of fourteenth century Europe. The only difference is that Russia ... will have time to bury its dead." This is part of a larger demographic trend in which wealthier economies are losing population and poorer economies are gaining.

Many Other Pressures on Boomers

Who was hurt more by the Great Recession—the Millennials or their parents? For the Boomers, hurt by corporate downsizing that has seen the gradual erosion of jobs their kind of middle management roles especially preserving their employment status has grown increasingly hard. We've known about this trend for more than 20 years; the *New York Times* reported on the disappearance of 43 million such jobs between 1979 and 1995—but the event was not some isolated trend of the Roaring 80s. It is with us even now as technology continues, ever relentlessly, to cut out the human element once known as the "middle man."

Aggravating this is globalization which—while certainly conveying benefits as well—has nonetheless taken jobs, first blue collar jobs, then white-collar employment. One perspective on this continuing complaint is the rise in age discrimination suits. They've risen by almost a third over the past decade or so—but so also have resolutions, with no discernible pattern to those resolutions.

Companies' move away from defined benefit pension schemes to defined contribution plans has also reduced retirement security while increasing vulnerability to market declines—such as the peak-to-bottom loss of 78 percent in the Dotcom bust of March 2000 to October 2002, or the broader S&P decline of 57 percent from its high of 1,576 in October 2007 to its low in March 2009 of 676. Between those abrupt and severe market declines, Boomers undertook to refinance their homes in record numbers. (In fact, between 2004 and 2007, more than half of Baby Boomers refinanced their homes, often to extract equity for other spending.) Our timing was not the best: interest rates were to drop to historic lows only *after* we had signed on those new dotted lines.

Together, these shifts have impaired Boomers' provision for retirement.

Given their reduced "employability," more and more are leaving the workforce permanently (another reason for the confusing picture presented by recent jobs numbers and a source of befuddlement to Federal Reserve policy-makers) or applying for (and receiving) disability payments (recipients now number one in eight of those in their late 50s). Some don't have a choice and must keep working—of those with a mortgage, 65 percent are still working at 64 (versus 54 percent of those who have paid off their homes).

For many, these circumstances go beyond sobering—one reason the suicide rate among Boomers is at record levels. The U.S. Center for Disease Control reports that since 1999, the suicide rate among males ages 45 to 54 years (a group including the youngest 50-plus Boomers) has continued to increase. In 2009, reports the CDC, the rate in the 45–54 group was 29.31 per 100,000, up 36.5 percent from 21.48 per 100,000 in 1999. Males ages 55 to 64 years (all Boomers) also made fatal choices in greater numbers. In 2009 the rate was up 32 percent from the rate in 1999 (from 19.78 in 1999 to 26.10 in 2009). In the same time period, the suicide rates among males ages 25 to 34 years and 35 to 44 years have remained more stable, increasing only 1.3 percent and 11.2 percent, respectively. Recall, however, from our earlier discussion, that those with unpaid debt had a higher rate. It seems that, sadly enough, our economic lives do affect our emotions. But read on, because there is hope for us all. Really.

CHAPTER 7

The Latest Intergenerational Heist: Obamacare

If you think healthcare is expensive now, wait until it's free.

—P.J. O'Rourke, author and political commentator

We have to pass the bill so that you can find out what is in it.

—House Speaker Nancy Pelosi, March 9, 2010,
urging passage of the Affordable Care Act

This bill was written in a tortured way to make sure CBO [the Congressional Budget Office] did not score the mandate as taxes. If CBO scored the mandate as taxes, the bill dies. Okay, so it's written to do that. In terms of risk-rated subsidies, if you had a law which said that healthy people are going to pay in—you made explicit healthy people pay in and sick people get money, it would not have passed. ... Lack of transparency is a huge political advantage. And basically, call it the stupidity of the American voter or whatever, but basically that was really, really critical for the thing to pass. ... Look, I wish Mark was right that we could make it all transparent, but I'd rather have this law than not.

—Jonathan Gruber, MIT professor and architect both of the
Affordable Care Act and Vermont's stillborn single-payer system,
Green Mountain Care. (Transcript of remarks made and video-recorded
at the University of Pennsylvania, October 2013)

T hough everyone seems to have a different estimate for the number of Americans lacking access to healthcare, it could be almost 50 million. But, Uncle Sam's latest "solution" won't work. Obamacare is just another "same old" big government band-aid based on tired and failure-ridden thinking that presumes good outcomes from bureaucrats rather than the free market—so it will have the opposite effect from its intention. To pay for it, Uncle Sam has his hand in your pocket again and this time, he REALLY needs you. Fortunately, there is a better way—and as usual, it's the only one we haven't tried.

Many years ago, I found myself stuck in downtown Manhattan traffic with Akio Morita, the co-founder of SONY. It was pouring rain and consequently we weren't moving very fast. Morita was not a patient man, and he struggled to retrieve something of value from this frustrating delay. He tried to make a phone call on one of those early mobile phones and it wasn't working well. His frustration mounting by the minute, he finally said, "We must invent portable music for time like this."

The idea took hold with him and not many months later, he hosted a big press conference to introduce the "Soundabout," soon rechristened the Walkman. It launched mobile music and became a huge success.

After that traffic delay, on his return to Tokyo, Morita had gone into the research department and, I'm sure, challenged them with something like, "Put music on wheels."

That's how, I was told many times, he also braced his technical people to invent the original video cassette recorder, the Betamax. Bored on one of the trans-Pacific flights he took so often, he strode into the R&D lab on his arrival and threw on the director's desk a paperback book.

"Put *Gone with the Wind* on a cassette that big," he'd commanded.

Morita, like other great leaders, knew how to put big, daunting challenges into metaphorical form and thus inspire people to overcome them. President Barack Obama took 1,700 pages to describe how he wanted to cover less than half those lacking healthcare insurance. And his administration has since added 7,000 additional pages of interpretations and regulations.

Any wonder why Obamacare appears to have failed? Barack is not Akio.

There are two sad truths to the Democrats' longtime effort to move toward a single payer, universal healthcare system. Whether we are talking about Hillarycare, the Health Security Act of 20-plus years ago, or today's

Obamacare, here is the sad truth:
- First, it was never going to work—i.e., provide that coverage OR bend the cost curve in healthcare. It was doomed from the start because it did absolutely nothing to encourage more rational use of our healthcare resources. It failed—even mocked—the power of the free market.
- Second, Millennials—America's young—were going to pay for it all along, for only by levying the increased cost against the young who don't use much healthcare could the government hope to pay for those who use it the most, the old.

Obamacare is, in fact, the most egregious example yet of government taking from the young to benefit the old.

And it has failed. Failed ugly amid swirling clouds of deceit and misrepresentation.

Specifically, you may recall these solemn pledges:
- "If you like your insurance plan, you can keep it."
- "If you like your doctor, there's no need to change."
- "Your premium will not go up."
- "It will not cost our economy any jobs."

All wrong. Totally discredited by actual experience.

Why Do So Many Government Efforts Fail?

"Hayek's greatest contribution to economics was to show that society is far more complex than we realize, with little pieces of knowledge dispersed among millions of individuals. 'The curious task of economics,' he famously wrote in the *The Fatal Conceit: The Errors of Socialism*, which he published in 1988, 'is to demonstrate to men how little they really know about what they imagine they can design.'

"Recent government interventions suggest that politicians and bureaucrats today think they can design just about anything. This ignorance has backfired, as it always does, bringing with it what economists call 'unintended consequences'.

"Consider the Affordable Care Act. The law's mandates, restrictions, prohibitions, taxes and subsidies are meant to make health insurance universally available. Yet since its passage in 2010, the proportion of Americans lacking health insurance has fallen only to 13 percent from 16 percent, according to a recent study by the Centers for Disease Control and Prevention. Millions of Americans have faced higher premiums, often losing their preferred doctors, contrary to what President Obama predicted and promised.

"Thanks to the hastily written law's incentives, Obamacare also has been a drag on employment. About 18 percent of employers surveyed by the Federal Reserve Bank of Philadelphia in August (2014) said that the ACA caused them to reduce the number of workers they employ."

—Donald J Boudreaux and Todd J. Zywicki, "A Nobel Economist's Caution
About Government", *Wall Street Journal*, October 2014

You might not have noticed, but by far a worse case of healthcare experimentation concluded in Vermont, the Left's laboratory, at the end of 2014. Like Obamacare, this effort envisioned the creation of a single payer, universal system, modeled on those of the U.K. and Canada.

Vermont made a recent and eye-opening effort to install such a system largely using Federal taxpayer money provided by the Obama administration. It took Vermont almost four years to figure out that two plus two equals four.

Vermont's Single Payer Washout

"Last week, in a reversal that deserves more attention, Democratic Governor Peter Shumlin announced that Vermont would no longer create America's first statewide single-payer health system. ...

"Single payer is the polite term for socialized medicine and the ultimate goal of the political left. ...

"Health and Human Services bestowed a $45 million grant for planning, and since 2011 Mr. Shumlin's team has worked closely with HHS, the Treasury and White House budget office.

"They hired William Hsaio of Harvard and Jonathan Gruber of MIT as policy architects. The former economist created Medicare's price controls in the 1980s and as for the latter, well, he's the guy who famously thinks you're stupid.

"Under the Vermont plan, all 625,000 state residents were to be automatically enrolled in the government plan, with the same benefits for all. As with Medicare, employers would be subject to a payroll tax that would reduce wages, and workers would pay a premium based on a sliding income scale. ...

"The state accountants estimated that his plan required an 11.5 percent tax on worker payroll, with no exceptions.

"Individuals, meanwhile, would have paid as much as 9.5 percent of earnings, which would have applied to everyone making more than four times the poverty level, or $102, 220 for a family of four—hardly the 1 percent. The full $2.59 billion in necessary funding would roughly double current state revenues (about $2.85 billion today).

"At least the Governor deserves credit for admitting failure. His ideological comrades are rarely dissuaded by the prospect of economic damage, as Obamacare proves."

—Lead editorial, *Wall Street Journal*, December 2014

The U.S. had a prospering healthcare industry that spawned innovation and was efficiently administered prior to the enactment of two major government programs, Medicare and Medicaid, in 1965. Innovation in insurance for healthcare promptly stopped.

Healthcare spending—3–5 percent of GDP for decades—has risen steadily since 1965 and now accounts of 17.4 percent of GDP. Though the rate of increase has slowed somewhat in recent quarters, few expect, hope as they may, such moderation to persist. In aggregate dollars, U.S. spending for healthcare in all its forms has risen from $27.4 billion in year 1960 to $2.9 trillion in 2013, with a growth rate consistently higher than GDP or the population growth.

Obamacare is a classic "same old" government approach, throwing taxpayer money at a problem and in the process, causing another, with little net benefit to society. To be sure, it addressed a legitimate shortcoming in our society—millions of Americans lacking access to healthcare insurance, about 13.4 percent of us, according to the Census (but much higher by others' reckoning)—but it turned out to be a wealth transfer, aka tax. So, it is just another subsidy, like its other healthcare cousins. Today, 50 million of us get subsidies from Medicare, 65 million more from Medicaid (the program for the disabled and poor), nine million from the scandal-ridden VA system, eight million for the Children's Health Insurance Program (or "CHIPS" for short; introduced in 1997, CHIPS covers kids whose families earn too much to qualify for Medicaid, but too little to afford private insurance. Since 1997, it has cut the uninsured rate for children in half—to 7 percent—at an annual cost of about $13 billion) and $10 million (and slowly growing) from Obamacare (or, more officially, and in fine oxymoronic fashion as mentioned, the Patient Protection and "Affordable" Healthcare Act).

Figure 10: Drop in Percentage of Uninsured Americans

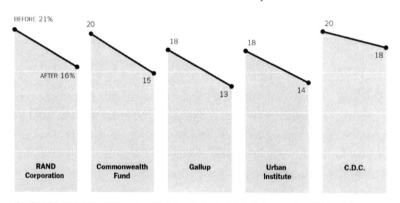

Five key surveys all show that the percentage of
uninsured Americans has declined in the last year

Note: For C.D.C., the "before" number is for all of 2013 and the "after" number is for the first three months of 2014. For all other surveys, the "before" numbers are for on or near the third quarter of 2013 and the "after" numbers are for the first six months of 2014.

Sources: Commonwealth Fund's Affordable Care Act Tracking Survey; RAND Health Reform Opinion Study; Urban Institute Health Reform Monitoring Survey; Gallup-Healthways Well-Being Index; Centers for Disease Control and Prevention's National Health Interview Survey

There is no clearer example than Medicare of how a concentrated benefit—this time bestowed on those over the age of 65—and its dispersed cost—to all taxpayers, especially the young—work to nourish special interest groups—in this case, the 37-million-member AARP, among others. Politicians fear few groups more. Among the reasons—old folks vote (unlike you Millennials).

Trust us—the Social Security mess is child's play compared to this one.

And the worst part is that the spending is not spread evenly throughout the population; it's weighted toward the generation of the politicians and the people who vote for them.

The pattern is familiar: An ill-conceived and immoral (can you call stealing from our kids to pay for our benefits anything else?) government program that is materially augmented by feckless officials (think Bush and the drug enhancement to Medicare), who—prodded by special interest groups and short-term political considerations—lie about its cost (think Gruber) and bureaucrats who multiply its complexity, then run it badly.

And it fails.

Dartmouth Medical School researchers have looked very carefully at Medicare spending. What have they found? About 30 percent of Medicare outlays do nothing to make beneficiaries healthier or happier.

Ambulance Chasers Favor Democrats by a Wide Margin

Oh—the other good news. Remember that $1 trillion-plus Medicare and Medicaid we mentioned earlier? Crooks are stealing a good 10 percent of that amount, an estimated $98 billion annually, through outright fraud (billing for nonexistent services) and "soft" fraud by hospital administrators and others who inflate bills through practices like "upcoding" (mischaracterizing a procedure so its reimbursement rate is higher). And let's not leave out the plaintiffs' bar, which stands ready to help you sue any medical professional. To shield themselves, doctors must not only buy expensive medical malpractice insurance, driving up their costs, but they also may make medical decisions in order to avoid liability—performing or refusing to perform certain tests or operations against their better medical judgment, for fear of being sued otherwise. It's proven very difficult to restrain this part of the bar or even get a "loser pays" provision installed to bring equity to this battlefield. We note without comment that the leading association for plaintiff lawyers—formerly called the Association of Trial Lawyers of America, but (in a blatant case of false labeling) recently rechristened as the American Association for Justice—donated 96 percent of their political contributions in 2014 to the Democratic Party, based on data released from the Federal Election Commission.

It's clear that a year or two from now, Obamacare will look very different.

At this point, however, we know several of its sponsors' earlier claims have been utterly discredited.

- In most cases, you can keep neither your existing insurance nor your present doctor.

- Most peoples' premiums are higher, not lower.
- It has pushed unemployment up, not down.
- The final cost is proving higher than forecast.
- Far fewer of the uninsured are enrolled than was predicted.
- A large new federal bureaucracy has begun to flourish in direct proportion to the program's continuing failure.

The basic reason Obamacare will prove another costly failure of well-intended government policy is simply this—it minimizes, even insults, the ability of the average citizen to do what's in his or her best interest, substituting an all-knowing but all-too-often inept crowd of government bureaucrats for the sound, collective judgment of the people. Call it the "hauteur of the liberal"—whose distinctive and utter confidence in government is exceeded only by their contempt for the citizens' intelligence.

So that's the bad news about healthcare. What's the good news, then? It turns out that there is a way to fix healthcare, temper its rising cost, and thereby broaden coverage. It is, in fact, the fastest-rising form of healthcare coverage in the state of Vermont, of all places, which recently abandoned its costly and ill-advised attempt to install a universal healthcare system in the state. Health savings accounts, matched with a high-deductible, low-cost catastrophic policy to cover things like cancer, are the best answer—especially for the young.

In fact, the average young couple, should they open such an account and experience average mortality and morbidity over their lives, will come to retirement age with almost a quarter of a million dollars in their HSAs—money that is theirs every step of the way, free of government mischief—money they can bequeath to their heirs.

Why do HSAs work so well? Simple—they put the power of the checkbook in the hands of the consumer, the only approach to healthcare cost containment that we haven't tried!

PART THREE

An America We Can Believe in Again

CHAPTER 8

Open Minds: The Challenge of Seeing the World as It Truly Is

We wear our opinions like a set of new clothes. Except—sadly—we don't change them as often. That has to change.

The most difficult subjects can be explained to the most slow-witted man if he has not formed any idea of them already; but the simplest thing cannot be made clear to the most intelligent man if he is firmly persuaded that he already knows, without a shadow of doubt, what is laid before him.

—Leo Tolstoy

Being a responsible adult is not easy—it's one reason why there are so few of them.

Scheduling discomfort—whether it's explaining how the dog ate your homework or having a tough conversation with a partner—is not easy. The same goes for deferring pleasure—it's a baby step from "Mommy, why can't I eat desert first?" to "I'll just put this on my credit card."

All of us—young or old—wrestle with those kinds of things.

There's another kind of dilemma—more sophisticated and more difficult. It's about how we reach conclusions about the complex world around us and how we distinguish between things. Dumb things and smart things.

Between good guys and bad guys. Attractive and unattractive ideas. About how we reach a point of view—one that reflects well on us and seems defensible and good for the world (after, of course, our self-interest is accounted for). It doesn't happen easily, the researchers tell us—especially when we observe or learn something that threatens our point of view; we hate to change our minds. It's hard to understand how smart people look at the same information and reach opposite conclusions.

> "No, the luckless product of our Liberal Universities, skill-less, will not touch that item his culture named taboo: work. So we see the proliferation, in the Liberal Communities, of counselors, advisors, life coaches, consultants, feng shui 'experts,' as the undereducated chickens some home to roost. ... They are inheriting a country bankrupted by their parents' spending. ...
> "There is an additional effect of the Liberal, learned aversion to actual work: the young 'practitioner' can exist only among his own. His specialized skills can be sold only in the Liberal Communities. He, thus, will quite literally never, cradle-to-grave, encounter a Conservative Idea, let alone a Conservative."
>
> —David Mamet, *The Secret Knowledge*

Why, for example, does one person come to describe himself as liberal while another self-identifies as a conservative? These native inclinations can be almost unfathomable—even to ourselves. How can both look at the same data and reach such contrary conclusions? How can either argue for a point of view that is totally contrary to the facts (not that facts are always so easy to find)—as we all do from time to time?

We've all heard words to the effect that, if a person is young and not a liberal, he lacks a heart; if he's old and not conservative, he lacks a brain. Attributed variously to Benjamin Disraeli, Winston Churchill, and George Bernard Shaw, the sentiment seems to hold true today, especially here in America, where we have the freedom to reject liberty, since we have it to some degree; some countries lack it altogether so long for it—think of the recent demonstrations in Hong Kong. As the voting proclivities described earlier make clear, the young (in the United States and elsewhere) vote liberal, frequently overwhelmingly so, just as Boomers generally take a more conservative stance. Thus, to look objectively at the accumulated data on the record of government programs and draw appropriate con-clusions, many of us—Millennials and Boomers alike—must put aside our native bias and *open our minds.*

THIS IS NEVER EASY FOR ANY OF US

Leon Festinger, a renown social scientist (and possible future Nobelist), explains why with his theories of social comparison and cognitive disso-nance. Best we, Millennial and Baby Boomer alike, understand it since it may clear the way to seeing the world the way it is, rather than how others might wish us to see it, and it will certainly help us present our views to others more effectively.

An earthquake in India inspired Festinger's theory of cognitive dis-sonance. Victims were terrified that an even bigger earthquake was im-minent, despite seismic evidence to the contrary. To Festinger, they accepted this to justify the fear that they felt still. Cognitive dissonance is the name he bestowed on the discomfort we feel holding two conflicting beliefs or having a belief challenged by new information (e.g., 'I believe in helping the less fortunate, so I hate the feeling that my support of the Living Wage leads to higher joblessness among young African Americans'). Smokers feel it, as does someone cheating on their spouse. The smoker, confronted with evidence that cigarettes cause lung cancer, may give up smoking (tough—nicotine is more addictive than crack cocaine), get new information (e.g., 'you can't prove that cancer link', for many years the malignant claim of The Tobacco Institute), or devalue the belief or attitude (i.e., better to enjoy life; que sera sera).

Festinger's social comparison theory posits that we test our ideas and beliefs against those of others and feel discomfort when they don't line up with those of friends and loved ones. We try to close those differences by changing their beliefs or our own. (This book is in part such an effort.)

In the book that resulted from Festinger's infiltration of a Doomsday cult, *When Prophecy Fails* (Harper-Torchbooks, 1956), he traced how a suburban housewife, claiming communication from the Guardians, aliens from another planet, said a flood would destroy the world on a certain day. Many cult members quit their jobs and sold their worldly goods. When the dreaded day arrived, but not the flood, the cult leader said the world had been spared because of the "force and good and light" the cult had spread. Rather than abandon their beliefs when thus confronted by new information, they instead proselytized with even more fervor!

How can this be? And what's it got to do with politics and public policy?

Bad beliefs are embraced more fervently when they are betrayed by new conflicting information when the belief is strongly held (as most political views are), are tied to behavior (something as simple as putting out a candidate's lawn signs, for example), has led to something that hard to undo (for the cult, jettisoning their jobs and possessions; for the citizen, restoring harmony after a bitter donnybrook at the family dinner table), and, among other things, when the challenged believer has support from the like-minded (other cult or party members). Hence, they will be even more ardent and that is self-enforcing.

Yes, change isn't easy.

But change we must.

In a superb survey of the research on how opinions form, change ("How Facts Backfire", *Boston Globe*, July 2010) or remain the same, despite new and compelling information, Joe Keohane challenges Thomas Jefferson's 1789 claim that "Whenever the people are well-informed, they can be trusted with their own government." Keohane summarizes the findings in this way: "Facts don't necessarily have the power to change minds. In fact, quite the opposite ... the problem is that sometimes the things they (voters) think they know are objectively, provably false. And in the presence of the correct information, such people react very, very differently than the merely misinformed ... they can entrench themselves even deeper."

This phenomenon, "backfire" to scholars, highlights the challenge of changing the minds of even the most influential of our fellow citizens. When we get information or anecdote, fact or hearsay, that confirms our position or view, we tend to retain it; but we reject evidence, however compelling, to the contrary. This is as true of political and other viewpoints as it is, for example, of how we approach investment decision-making (serious cautions there, folks). Professionals call this "confirmation bias" and there's only one way to deal with it—keep hurling credible data at it.

Sadly, researchers have found that misinformed people have the strongest political opinions—whether the issue is welfare, education, healthcare reform, affirmative action, or gun control, among others.

This "often wrong, but never in doubt" pattern makes it very hard to move anyone off badly-formed views. Partly, it's defensiveness; where self-esteem is high, however, the mind is more open to new information and to change.

We Need 'Truth Squads' in 2016

Brendan Nyhan, a leading researcher in these areas at the University of Michigan, suggests increasing the "reputational risk" of putting out bad information by calling out the guilty, but Keohane is not optimistic that this "shaming" technique will change things. I disagree. When one party or another makes a major TV address, I like that the opposing party then offers an immediate rejoinder; in fact, I wish the fact-checking could happen so fast that outright lies could be made known right then. I'd like it even more if fact-checking "truth squads" followed candidates around and posted their findings on readily-accessible-to-all web sites like ours (www.tinfl.org).

Changing the world may simply begin with each of us learning how to ask three simple questions. When we encounter someone with a differing point of view—and this relates clearly to public policy issues, but to our most intimate relationships as well—we could dismiss them out of hand for being uninformed, short-sighted or simply unthinking; or, we might reach into the therapist's bag of tricks (and, after all, their fundamental goal is to help patients better understand and, when appropriate, change their behavior) by asking three questions.

Questions like these:
- "I'd like to understand how you feel about this. Please tell me your point of view."
- "I'd also like to know how you came to feel this way."
- "Okay. I think I understand how you feel about this now. But I'd like to be sure. My sense is that ... ." (Repeat to be sure you do get it.)

Take your time. Listen attentively. Ask follow-up questions. We all want to be heard and to be understood. And we will adhere to our position until we are. New, compelling facts don't matter. We are talking here about human nature.

When you feel you understand how the other person reached his point of view, and he's confirmed that you do, then—and only then—you can say, "I've tried to understand how you feel about this. And I think we can agree that I do. Would you care to hear how I personally view this matter?"

Then, tell 'em.

The "eureka" moment, if you get one, can't mean or imply that "You were an idiot before." And don't forget, insight doesn't change behavior necessarily, but it can help us to understand and accept our mistakes—though even this may not change behavior.

We All Know a Virtucrat
and Some of Us May Even Be One

Joseph Epstein, a prolific essayist and editor of The American Scholar, Phi Beta Kappa's magazine, for many years, coined the term "virtucrat" to describe a subset—those whose inflated self-esteem rests on the virtuousness of their opinions, of which none are more vital to this self-image than their political views. They cross the political spectrum from left to right, with "the liberal virtucrat for social justice, security, innovation; the conservative virtucrat for liberty, enterprise, tradition. The former considers the latter heartless, the latter considers the former naïve."

In a recent article ("After the Midterms, Virtucrats Still Rule", *Wall Street Journal*, November 2014), Epstein notes that "The virtucrat is nothing if not Manichean. For him there is right and there is wrong, and he is, invariably and inevitably, solidly in the right. Those who do not believe as he does are not merely wrong, but stupid, foolish and, when you get right down to it, scum, really. The English mathematician and philosopher Alfred North Whitehead wrote in 1920: 'Seek simplicity and distrust it.' The virtucrat, liberal or conservative, finds simplicity and is entirely comfortable with it."

Epstein cautions that changing a virtucrat's views is tough. "How could it be otherwise," he asks, "so long as the virtucrat views his own position as unassailable and yours as more or less immoral?

"Political arguments at the level of ideology are seldom won. As Jonathan Swift wrote: 'It is useless to attempt to reason a man out of a thing he wasn't reasoned into.' None of us has been reasoned into his politics. We came by them through the indirect influence of family, friends, and social and economic position: sometimes in consonance with these influences, sometimes in reaction against them. Politics is a great many things, but reasonable has never been chief among them," Epstein concludes.

CHAPTER 9

We Have to Smarten Up

What's "fair"? Nothing is absolute—it's about trade-offs. The issues that matter to Millennials are mostly social*—choice, climate/ environment, gender equality, racial justice, among others, but the* economic *ones—taxes, government spending, entitlements, income redistribution, minimum/"living" wage, for example—are* really *important. Think clearly about them.*

> *The next time some academics tell you how important diversity is, ask how many Republicans there are in their sociology department.*
>
> —Thomas Sowell

E very poll shows that Millennials care deeply about their world, especially about the disadvantaged. This leaves them vulner- able to exactly the kind of emotional appeals that encrust the most divisive issues of our time—and both parties know how to strum this guitar. We need to ignore those emotional appeals and parse the often-conflicting views we encounter to find the truth about these issues.

There are many ways, for example, to reduce income inequality—ag- gravated of late by the rich participating in the stock market recovery, which the less well off failed to do. History shows that the best way is through growth, which lifts everyone. Sadly, in today's environment, growth is slow and governments are reluctant to increase their deficits—by spending for infrastructure, for example, which is badly needed in the U.S. and elsewhere in the developed world. That leaves the stage open for populist notions like higher taxes (especially from the rich)—even though this generally suppresses growth.

No one speaks with more clarity to this challenge of determining right and wrong and, importantly, "fair", than Stephen Moore, now of the Heritage Foundation, formerly an editorial page staffer of the *Wall Street Journal*. In countless books and articles, Moore has argued the rational approach to the challenges of our time—and nowhere more effectively than in his 2012 book on what "fairness" truly means when the smoke of partisan debate is dispelled.

"The issue is: How do we make sure that the middle class and the poor can get ahead and address societal shortcomings? The left argues that conservatives don't care about poor people, and this is why they oppose income redistribution to the poor, higher budgets for social programs, regulations like higher minimum wages, and so on.

"But one of the premises of this book is that it is equally (maybe even more) plausible to say that liberals don't care about poor people. The welfare state has trapped generations in poverty. Liberals opposed welfare reform when it was a great success in lifting the incomes of the poor. (Author's Note: In the years immediately following President Clinton's welfare reform in 1996, the rolls of welfare recipients shrank by 50 percent.) High tax rates are not an effective way to redistribute income. The minimum wage eliminates jobs for those at the bottom. The left defends inner city schools, but those dismally performing schools have done as much as anything to hold back the economic progress of the poor. The dissolution of the black family, in part because of welfare, has forced several generations of black children to be reared in fatherless homes, which is a prescription for trouble later in life. Solve these thorny problems and you go a long way toward solving the inequality."

—Stephen Moore, *Who's The Fairest Of Them All?*

Most liberals, for example, take pride in their sensitivity to the needs of the disadvantaged—they feel that this makes them different than conservatives. And they are certainly more supportive of government programs that appear—hold that thought—to provide for the less successful in our midst. Conservatives, on the other hand, distrust government—they find it all-too-often inept and inefficient. Occasionally even corrupt.

On a more personal basis, when one looks, for example, at facts on individual philanthropy a somewhat different picture emerges—conservatives are much more generous with their own money than liberals are with theirs. Liberals are generous with *our* money.

'THE GREAT TURNING POINT' AS PETE PETERSON SEES IT

I first became acquainted with Peter Peterson, former chairman of Lehman Bros., (when it thrived well before the 2008 bankruptcy), and cofounder of the Blackstone Group, as a member of The Economic Club of New York, a forum before which world figures regularly appear to make often-significant policy statements and which Peterson chaired with wit and grace for a time. Since then, I've followed his concern—as expressed through countless speeches, articles, books and other involvements, including that of his eponymous foundation, The Peterson Institute—for our future with close interest. A fabulously successful entrepreneur, he is a tireless and objective advocate for sane government and for our children, whose inheritance he sees government squandering through ill-advised, selfish and poorly conceived and administered programs. In his 2004 book, *Running on Empty*, he points to where the U.S. lost its way.

> "What gave rise to our recent bipartisan flight from fiscal integrity—and when? I believe that most of it happened during the 'Me Decades' of the mid-Sixties to the mid-Eighties when a socially fragmenting America began to gravitate around a myriad of interest groups, each more fixated on pursuing and financing its own agenda than on safeguarding the common good of the nation. Political parties, rather than transcend the fissures and bind the country together, instead began to cater to them and ultimately sold themselves out. Along the way, they sold posterity out as well."

In his analysis, Peterson divides the period into two periods, each dominated by one of the major political parties.

> "First came the decade of 1964 to 1973, full of optimism and hubris about what the public sector could accomplish, when people talked about how much more everyone ought to get from government. This was the high tide of the benefit expansion, led by an ascendant Democratic Party. Then came the decade of 1974 to 1983, full of skepticism about the public sector and a growing faith in markets, when people talked about how much less anyone ought to give to government. This was the high tide of the tax revolt, led by an ascendant Republican Party. Both parties today celebrate icons from these periods (Lyndon Johnson and his 'Great Society' for the Democrats; Ronald Reagan and his 'Opportunity Society' for the Republicans) as a way to distinguish themselves from the other side."

Liberals also express more confidence in government's ability to help people (though with public confidence in Congress so low—14 percent just weeks before the 2014 mid-term elections—it's hard to detect much confidence at all). This despite a long and continuing litany of failure in virtually every major program the government has undertaken.

SNOW JOB OF THE CENTURY—THE '30S FED CONVINCES US THEY SAVED AMERICA FROM THE DEPRESSION THEY CAUSED

Milton Friedman traces this bias in favor of government solutions to the Great Depression: it "was the overwhelmingly important event that persuaded the public that government could do good. ... It is ironic that the Great Recession was produced by government but was blamed on the private enterprise system. The Federal Reserve System explained in the 1933 annual report how much worse things would have been if the Federal Reserve had not behaved so well, yet the Federal Reserve was the chief culprit in making the depression as deep as it was." Public attitudes changed as a result. "It is interesting to note," Friedman adds, "that every economic plank of the 1928 Socialist party platform has by now been either wholly or partly enacted."

Even Roosevelt's much-esteemed Treasury secretary, Henry Morgenthau, was skeptical of the New Deal—but privately. Writing in his private diary, he noted, "we have tried spending money. We are spending more than we have ever spent before and it does not work. ... We have never made good on our promises. ... I say after eight years of this Administration we have just as much unemployment as when we started ... and an enormous debt to boot!"

To many the answer to our problems is simply to take from those who have and give to those who do not. The fancy word is redistribution. It is a central theme among the left. Just look at how Senator Elizabeth Warren would relieve the student loan crisis—"close loopholes for millionaires and billionaires." The logical follow-up questions include: What loopholes? And, if you can find some, how much will that raise? And is reducing already-low education borrowing costs the best use of that money? And, by the way, the debt wouldn't be so big if colleges could achieve some productivity instead of cheerfully and with impunity raising their prices— raising them much faster than any other product/service provider in the country. Sadly, the media too-seldom follows up with that kind of inquiry.

MR. PIKETTY'S GLARING OMISSION

In an ironic twist, given that his home country is France, Thomas Piketty is a prominent voice today on income inequality which France has fought with a wide variety of socialist programs what have mostly succeeded in suppressing growth. Piketty's 2014 *New York Times* best-seller (with Emmanuel Saez), *Capital In The Twenty-First Century*, traces the wealth and income inequality they see here and in Europe for more than two centuries. (There's more irony—a European telling America how to run the strongest economy in the world.) Paul Krugman praised the volume in *The New York Review of Books* as a "magnificent, sweeping meditation on inequality." In their book, they argue that in such developed economies, the return on capital typically surpasses the rate of economic growth (the equation looks like this: "R>G") and hence 'the rich get richer'. Ultimately, such gaps could erode and jeopardize our democratic foundations, they fear; thus we must close those gaps for everyone's benefit, by "redistributing" income and wealth—through more progressive taxes, for example. The American left cherishes such an idea as, we may presume, does France's socialist premier Hollande, to whom Piketty acts as an advisor (though to little apparent effect since President Hollande's approval rating in France slid to 12 percent at the end of 2014, mostly due to disapproval of his handling of economic issues). Oh—Piketty also purports to prove that the Laffer Curve effect—so clearly demonstrated in the U.S. under Presidents Kennedy, Reagan and Clinton, has no effect in France.

There's just one (well, maybe more than one) problem with Piketty's approach and it goes to the very heart of his case: in calculating household incomes and wealth, he fails to include the very remedies he proposes—transfer payments, which have grown bigger and bigger over past decades, especially in France.

This wasn't missed by other scholars. Just a minute, say economists Philip Armour and Richard V. Burkhauser of Cornell, and Jeff Larrimore of Congress's Joint Committee on Taxation. They expanded the Piketty/Saez definition of income to include, logically enough, precisely those things like Social Security payments, government medical insurance and changes in tax policy that Piketty recommends to redress income inequality. This more inclusive approach destroys Piketty's central claim, dramatically restaging the national debate on inequality.

Michael Solon, budget advisor to new majority leader Mitch McConnell, summarized the changes in a November 2014 *Wall Street Journal* article co-authored with Phil Gramm, former Texas Republican senator:

> "The bottom quintile of Americans experienced a 31 percent increase in income from 1979 to 2007 instead of a 33 percent decline that is found using a Piketty-Saez market-income measure alone. The income of the second quintile, often referred to as the working class, rose by 32 percent, not 0.7 percent. The income of the middle quintile, America's middle class, increased by 37 percent, not 2.2 percent."

Even Piketty himself, writing in the *American Economic Review*, now says his theory doesn't relate to the last century: "I do not view R>G as the only or even the primary tool for considering changes in income and wealth in the 20th century or for forecasting the path of inequality in the 21st century." Further, he acknowledges that "wealth inequality is currently much less extreme than a century ago."

Data like this should give pause to the demagogues on the Left who see inequity where it doesn't exist to justify their positions (which inevitably and inexorably press for more government and higher welfare outlays).

Gramm and Solon acknowledge in their article that "income is 24 percent less equally distributed here than in the average of the other 34 member countries of the OECD. But OECD figures show that U.S. per capita GDP is 42 percent higher, household wealth is 210 percent higher and median disposable income is 42 percent higher." How many Americans, they ask, "would give up 42 percent of their income to see the rich get less?"

Progressives Seem to Have it All Wrong on Inequality

Progressives like Elizabeth Warren demonize the 1 percent of highest earners (and the high multiple of average worker paychecks that are bestowed on some corporate CEO's—in some cases, 300 or higher).

"We must narrow the gap between the rich and poor, change how wealth and income are allocated and bring justice to our society," they demand.

I don't know how much of their large incomes the Warrens or the Clintons give to the less advantaged (though we do know that Republicans in fact give more of their own money away to charities than do Democrats), but this central theme of taking from the rich and giving to the less-advantaged has bipartisan appeal to most Americans, including those very rich ones (many of whom have already pledged to do so by bequeathing their wealth to charities of their choice).

But is unconditional generosity good policy?

Actually, no. It's bad policy. And demagogues reviling the richest among us as the cause of The Inequality Problem can thwart its rational solution.

Here's why.

The OECD (Organization for Economic Cooperation and Development, a 34-nation group that seeks to "improve the economic and social well-being of people around the world") has taken a deep look at income inequality. Their latest—*In It Together: Why Less Inequality Benefits All*—argues that inequality depresses GDP growth; in fact, the report asserts, the increase in income inequality in the twenty years after 1985 reduced GDP growth globally by 4.7 percent between 1990 and 2010.

Unlike the demagogues, however, they say those billionaires are NOT the problem; the problem is the inequality between the middle class and the lowest earners—and their recommendations are to improve schools that serve low-income families and boost wage subsidies (like the earned income tax credit or EITC). Do that, the report argues, and we will shrink the vast wasted potential of those at the bottom of the economic ladder.

Note the conflict, however. To fix inner city schools—for example, by offering parents choice through vouchers, charter schools and the like— would pit liberal politicians against entrenched special interests like the teachers unions. Think elected officials like union water-boy and NYC mayor Bill deBlasio would ever go for that?

See the problem?

"Fair" is a word fraught with very different meaning to different people.

Stephen Moore puts "fair" in perspective. Here are just a few of the issues he raises early in his book, *Who's The Fairest Of Them All?*

- Is it fair that federal employees receive pay and benefits that are nearly double the pay and benefits of the private sector workers who pay their salaries?
- Is it fair that big banks got huge government subsidies because they bought trillions of mortgage-backed securities, but the smaller community banks they compete against got nothing?
- Is it fair that we compel tens of millions of young people in America to pay 12 percent of every paycheck into a Social Security system that is running out of money and is likely to offer these workers a negative rate of return on their investment?
- Is it fair that 90 percent of the reporters who are covering the presidential election are Democrats?
- Is it fair that the three counties that have the highest per capita income in America are all inside the Washington, D.C. metropolitan area?
- Is it fair that soon almost half of the federal budget will take income from young, working people and redistribute it to old, nonworking people that as a group have higher incomes?
- Is it fair that in twenty-seven states workers can be compelled to join a union if they want to keep their job?

- Is it fair that nearly four out of 10 American households now pay no federal income tax at all?

Let's assume that we double the tax on the richest 3 percent of Americans who presently provide 97 percent of total tax revenue. It doesn't take a genius to see that doesn't balance a fiscal deficit as large as ours—much less fortify the rapidly eroding finances of Social Security and Medicare.

So let's triple, even quadruple that tax. We're still billions short. The rich have the ability, which most of us don't share, of timing their income; raise the tax rate and they will defer recognizing taxable income—and their lifestyle won't change.

Raising taxes—read my lips—to restore prosperity, build "fairness" etc.—is the modern equivalent of medieval bloodletting. It does not work and it is killing us.

Why the Minimum Wage Could Be the Most Racist Policy in America

This may shock you, but the minimum or "living" wage is arguably the most racist of our failed public policies. Here's why.

The minimum wage traces to the Industrial Revolution, when—like today's post-Recession America—a large disparity opened up between workers and the fabulously wealthy capitalists who built our railroads, auto, steel, oil and other industries. Their names are well-known—Rockefeller, Carnegie, Mellon, Ford, Bessemer. (We get the word "sabotage" from the Industrial Revolution's early days in Holland, where threatened workers threw their "sabots" or shoes into the new machines.)

Another factor was the ubiquity of child labor. As Thomas E. Hall notes in *Aftermath: The Unintended Consequences Of Public Policies*, in 1900 more than one million children worked, often in dreadful conditions and for very low wages. Unions favored the minimum wage idea in hopes that employers would replace children (and women) with male union members.

Starting in Massachusetts in 1912, many states passed a minimum wage law, usually relating only to the employment of women and children. In 1923, the Supreme Court struck the laws down and the issue was lost in the ensuing boom of the 1920s, only to be resurrected in the Depression, with its soaring joblessness. The 1938 Fair Labor Standards Act made it federal law, but to little effect as war intervened. This changed in 1956 when the minimum hourly wage was raised from 75 cents to $1 and the Department of Labor was authorized to monitor compliance.

And what did that surveillance reveal? A big surge in 16-year-old unemployment, *especially among black 16-year-olds.*

Between 2007 and 2009 in a move that affirmed the government's lame sense of timing, the minimum wage was raised in three steps from $5.15 to $7.25 and again, teenage employment declined significantly. About 15.5 percent pre-Recession, it reached 27.1 percent in December 2009—the highest level since 1948. Again, the effect was disproportionately high among black teenagers!

Unions like to cloak their support for the minimum wage with humanitarian concern; nonsense. Unions support such hikes in hopes that higher required wage rates will mean more jobs for their skilled union members.

"Since the reality is that a significant proportion of workers actually earning the minimum wage are teenagers or young adults living with their parents, many argue that the minimum wage law doesn't actually cause much damage. Yet the effects of high unemployment among this demographic group should not be discounted. One reason is that the lack of employment opportunities for young people deprives them of valuable work experience in the form of learning the responsibility of showing up for a job on time, learning to follow directions and complete tasks, learning to work with others, and dealing with (sometimes) disagreeable bosses. These skills can prove to be beneficial later in life.

"Even more pernicious, perhaps, is the result found by a number of studies that a higher minimum wage causes some U.S. teenagers to drop out of high school and instead seek jobs paying the higher wage. This consequence is clearly detrimental, not just to the youths but to society as well, and certainly not what minimum wage supporters thought would happen. In addition, unemployed youths (especially males) who are not attending school are much more likely to impose costs on society by committing crimes and becoming involved in the criminal justice system.

"Raising unemployment, promoting racial discrimination in the workplace, increasing the high school dropout rate, and raising the incidence of crime by youths are unintended consequences of the minimum wage law. Do minimum wage advocates really support these goals?"

—Thomas E. Hall, *Aftermath* (Cato Institute, 2014)

IF THE U.S. EDUCATION SYSTEM WERE A BUSINESS, IT WOULD BE BANKRUPT

Of most immediate consequence to them—having already suffered the ill effect of minimum wage laws when they went looking for after-school part-time employment and found opportunity lacking (though not perhaps understanding one reason why), is the broken U.S. educational system.

As any Millennial can tell you, higher education costs too much, fails to leverage advanced technology, has little concern about productivity (and offers scant evidence that it can achieve it) and has been bureaucratized like the government itself—which has aided all these negative outcomes. The cruelest outcome is that the poor and disadvantaged—to whom education in a most American way offers hope of advance—are hurt the most by education's drift toward costly mediocrity.

The facts tell the story. A recent OECD study reveals the U.S., second in 2000 in the share of the population with a college degree, is now fifth. Among 25–34-year-olds, globally, we're twelfth.

The problem isn't the teachers' work ethic—our college teachers work longer hours than their overseas peers, though they earn less. And the results of a college degree appear to be diluting, as two books by Richard Arum and Joseph Rossa show: more than a third of graduates made no progress in critical thinking or analytical reasoning over the four years. In an even bigger survey—of 1,600 students (Class of 2009) at twenty-five colleges—they found that the average student spent 12–14 hours studying each week. (didn't we Baby Boomers spend that on some days?) These same students found the transition to adult life challenging—except those who, like the typical foreign student, studied practical subjects like business, science, math, engineering and the like. This recalls what the English major asks of the engineering grad in a restaurant: "You want fries with that?" But, it's no laughing matter.

Education Innovation Is Coming From the Free Market

Government's role, if any, should be to encourage and cheerlead reform and experimentation; yet it thwarts both. To date, there is no evidence that elevating education to cabinet-level stature (as candidate Jimmy Carter did to win support of the teachers' unions) has yielded any benefit at all. The real innovations are coming, as they so often do, from the free market—firms like Udacity and Coursera, for-profit startups offering online courses featuring the best professors (think of those Great Lectures brochures you get in the mail) from the best institutions.

Such experimentation has shown that MOOCs ("Massive Open Online Courses") can provide what Jeffrey J. Selingo, author of *MOOC U: Who's Getting the Most Out Of Online Education*, calls "just-in-time education". He points out that, "The MOOC provides learning in chunks, at a student's pace." And cheaper.

Like a health savings account does for healthcare, MOOCs put control in the hands of the consumer every step of the way. You choose the "what, where and when" of your learning—and you get it from the best teachers in the world.

Bob Kerrey, ex-governor and Senator and ex-president of the New School, is another innovator. The Minerva Project with which he's associated combines online education with small classes and personal attention to students (who live in dorms). The goal? An Ivy League-quality result at half the price. As CNBC's Becky Quick points out, "Minerva doesn't have to lease or own as much classroom space, and if it can archive the best lectures and courses, the school's labor costs go down."

A word about vocational education, where too the Internet can slash costs, enabling the student to learn while working. According to a recent McKinsey survey ("Education to Employment: Getting Europe's Youth Into Work"), half of the young people surveyed in four of the seven countries would have preferred a vocational field of study. There's additional and good reason for the attention—20 percent unemployment among Europe's youth (versus 15 percent in the U.S.).

Clayton Christensen, of Harvard Business School, and Michelle Weise, of the Christensen Institute, argue in a new book that MOOCs are not the answer, but a new approach to learning will be one, as *The Economist* noted recently, that "makes plenty of use of the Internet but ties education more closely to work. The emphasis on competences rather than subjects will make vocational education better suited to post-industrial economies. It will also challenge the dominance of universities as students realize that they no longer have to amass huge debts in order to acquire marketable skills."

Like the minimum wage, racial preferences as applied to education have demonstrably hurt minorities (though not Senator Elizabeth Warren, who invoked such a preference when she applied to Harvard claiming Native American status).

As Jason Riley points out:

> Members of the US Commission on Civil Rights have noted that "extreme empirical research indicating that students who attend schools where their entering academic credentials put them in the bottom of the class are less likely to follow through with an ambition to major in science and engineering than similarly credentialed students who attend schools where their credentials put them in the middle or top of the class. Affirmative action then works to the detriment of the supposed beneficiaries."

'Do-the-Math' Environmentalists Have Trouble With Counting

Another hot issue for the young is the environment and it is here that their sense of stewardship, more pronounced and sincere perhaps than that of the Baby Boomers, resonates. Environmental concern embraces many related issues: global warming, climate change, carbon footprint and many more. And here we find many of the Left's favorite high priests—people like Bill McKibben of "do the math" fame.

Permit this writer to get irresponsibly anecdotal for a moment. I live in Florida part of the winter and I live on the water. To set the alarmist mood, note that I live in the FLOOD ZONE! And I live here happily. It's been nine years since the last hurricane. And, near as I can tell, the water level isn't rising. Yes—it's nice and warm here in the winter, but I know that the global temperatures haven't increased much in fifteen years (.09 percent to be exact, 90 percent lower than most models predicted), so I don't fear unbearably hot winters. Maybe all those extreme proposals to reduce man-made effects on the climate were—dare I say—a little over the top? Especially so, given that the less advantaged would have disproportionately borne the costs of Al Gore's paranoia. Like McKibben suggests, do the math.

Better yet, perhaps, administer a lie detector test. All too often, zealots bend the truth. A good example is described by John McClaughry, founder of Vermont's Ethan Allen Institute. This from their blog:

12-12-14—ANOTHER ENVIRONMENTAL FALSEHOOD

"A week ago Citizens Climate Lobby 'group leader' Rick Wackernagel published a piece in the *Burlington* (Vermont) *Free Press* trying to sell Vermonters on a carbon tax.

"In it, he repeated that '97 percent of active climate scientists agree that global warming is real, serious, and caused mainly by human activity.'

"This number originated with a quickie survey of 10,257 earth scientists. The two University of Illinois researchers excluded the solar and space scientists, cosmologists, physicists, meteorologists and astronomers who might have thought that the sun and planetary movements might have something to do with Earth's climate. They reduced the initial list to 3,146 who responded to these two questions:
- When compared with pre-1800s levels, do you think that mean global temperatures have generally risen, fallen, or remained relatively constant?
- Do you think human activity is a significant contributing factor in changing mean global temperatures?

"Ninety percent of the respondents answered 'risen' to the first question, presumably assuming it referred to the pre-1850 Little Ice Age. Eighty-two percent of the respondents answered 'yes' to the second question.

"Those percentages weren't impressive enough, so the researchers reduced the sample until only 77 remained. Seventy-five of them said 'yes' to both questions, producing the desired 'consensus' finding that '97 percent of "active climate researchers" believe that humans are a significant cause of global warming.'

"This manufactured 'consensus' is obviously dishonest, and it won't be the last bit of dishonesty offered up by the carbon tax advocates."

One of my central themes is the unintended consequences of government action—action often provoked by alarmists who sometimes—God forbid!—bend the facts to serve their sense of apocalyptic catastrophe. Better, we say, to focus on growth of the kind that lifts all boats, especially that of the disadvantaged. So, too, we'd argue when it comes to global warming.

Bjorn Lomborg, author of *The Skeptical Environmentalist* (Cambridge Press, 2001), is director of the Copenhagen Consensus Center and a leading analyst of the climate debate. In a recent article, he argued for a more even-handed view of the climate debate.

"... if we want to help the poor people who are most threatened by natural disasters, we have to recognize that it is less about cutting carbon dioxide emissions that it is about pulling them out of poverty.

"The best way to see this is to look at the world's deaths from natural disasters over time. In the Oxford University database for death rates from floods, extreme temperatures, droughts and storms, the average in the first part of last century was more than 13 dead every year per 100,000 people. Since then the death rates have dropped 97 percent to a new low in the 2010s of 0.38 per 100,000 people.

"The dramatic decline is mostly due to economic development that helps nations withstand catastrophes. If you're rich like Florida, a major hurricane might cause plenty of damage to expensive buildings, but it kills few people and causes a temporary dent in economic output. If a similar hurricane hits a poorer country like the Philippines or Guatemala, it kills more and can devastate the economy.

"In short, climate change is not worse than we thought. Some indicators are worse, but some are better. That doesn't mean that global warming is not a reality or not a problem. It definitely is. But the narrative that the world's climate is changing from bad to worse is unhelpful alarmism, which prevents us from focusing on smart solutions."

—"The Alarming Thing About Climate Alarmism",
Wall Street Journal, February 2015.

May I Have Another Helping of Frankenfood Please?

When it gets humid in Florida, we return to Vermont, where the legislature recently passed—in another example of Vermont's "narcissistic altruism"—the country's first mandatory GMO licensing bill (two more were on the ballot in November, in Oregon and Colorado, but lost). Labeling bills have been introduced in another 26 states—leading some to speculate that this will ultimately lead to federal licensing, somewhat like the national law requiring calorie detail on labels. (Some fear that such success could lead to all manner of new demands—for example, a food product's carbon footprint.) Vermont's version is scheduled to go into effect in 2016, if it survives a court challenge.

The slogans sounded reasonable at the time Vermont's lawmakers debated the measure—"we have the right to know", "how can transparency hurt?" and so forth. Reasonable enough, one might suppose. But such requirements have costs—millions, some say, to effect compliance—and these were largely ignored. Such costs take the form of higher costs to the producers, who must in turn reflect the costs in their prices; in less supply, as some producers decide it isn't worth it to sell their wares in a small market such as Vermont; and in liability to the trial lawyers' mischief (though truth be told the plaintiff bar isn't as ubiquitous in Vermont as elsewhere).

Millennials—you've been eating genetically modified food your entire lives. Mankind has been eating "Frankenfood" for centuries, for millennia. And now, virtually everyone who produces food, if they are true to the spirit of this over-arching statute, must declare that their product has been genetically-modified because the labeling law effectively replaces the process guarantee commonly associated with organic food with a product guarantee that is impossible to warrant since it is the very nature of plants that their seeds propagate far and wide. For example, 90 percent of U.S. corn and soybean production is of genetically-modified crops.

This all means higher cost to the consumer and probably less choice and availability, as some producers opt out of the required compliance. *This—even though there has never been a single instance of someone's health suffering from such food.*

Soon, too, you will see the unintended consequences of the new law as the organic farmers, of which there are many in Vermont, almost all of whom supported the GMO labeling bill, come to realize—perhaps prodded by a lawsuit or two from the plaintiff bar alleging, on behalf of all Vermont consumers, mislabeling—that their organic food products contain GMO's. And, likely, they do.

Makes you wonder what Vermont's legislators were thinking, doesn't it?

War on Women?

Do women make less? Is there, as liberals often charge, a (Republican-led) "War on Women"?

Conventional wisdom holds that women are paid less than men in equivalent jobs—sometimes significantly less. True or false?

The answer appears to be a *little less*—but even a little less, we'd agree, is too much.

In 2009, the Labor Department commissioned an analysis of more than 50 studies on this and found, as Kate Batchelder has pointed out in the *Wall Street Journal* (October 2014, "The Top Ten Liberal Superstitions"), that "the so-called pay gap "may be almost entirely" the result of choices both men and women make." That is, those who would ascribe a lack of fairness to the sexes' "different pay fail to account for career field, education or personal choices. When those factors are included, the wage gap disappears." For example, not too many women aspire to a career as a logger (the most dangerous job in America) or truck driver. And high pay isn't nearly as important to most women as it is to most men. Males are more likely to work in less desirable locations—and get paid for that; they work longer hours, too—on average—and are more likely to work on weekends. They also favor high-stress jobs and those requiring more specialization. Unmarried women who don't have children actually earn more than unmarried men, according to author Marty Nemko, who relied on data gleaned from the Census Bureau.

Note the key language above—"may be almost"; it certainly does NOT explain the disparity between gender (or race) wage rates which others observe. The difference one most frequently hears, one based on raw wage data, is about 78 percent (more for women of color), that such discrimination characterizes nearly every occupation, and grows larger with age.

The U.S. Department of Labor studied this exhaustively and concluded that there are observable differences in the attributes of man and women that account for most of the wage gap (more time off for family caregiving by women; more hazardous occupations for men, as noted above). Statistical analysis that includes these variables has produced results that collectively account for between 65.1 and 76.4 percent of a raw gender gap of 20.4 percent, and thereby leave an adjusted gender wage gap that is between 4.8 and 7.1 percent—a residual that comes up in others' research as well. Some ascribe this wage differential to discrimination, citing studies where replacing a woman's name with a man's on a resume led to a salary reduction. The Department of Labor, however, fails to concur with this speculation. Conclusion: based on these and other research findings, it appears that wage discrimination against women has declined (in some studies, very significantly), but some stubbornly remains, its precise origins tough to pinpoint and thus to remedy.

Federal law prohibits such discrimination. But enforcement relies on victims' asserting their claims, which they are often understandably reluctant to do. The U.S. Government Accountability Office (GAO) has found, after studying compliance, that the Equal Employment Opportunity Commission and Department of Labor "should better monitor their performance in enforcing anti-discrimination laws."

OPEN SEASON ON THE MIDDLE CLASS?

Are we killing the middle class, as many proclaim, looking at how income inequality has grown in recent years?

Clearly, the economy's shift from brawn to brains, and capital for labor, abetted by the Internet and increasing use of technology, has benefitted the better-educated and increased inequality.

Economists can measure this through the Gini coefficient; it computes the ratio of top incomes relative to low incomes. The Gini coefficient ranges between 0 (perfect equality—everyone has an equal share) and 1.0 (perfect inequality—some greedy bastard has it all). Thus, the higher the ratio, the more pronounced the inequality. No question, it's been rising.

The Census Bureau also computes Gini coefficents for each state, so we can trace where income is rising and falling—another measure of how effective some states have been in reducing such inequality.

Stephen Moore and Richard Vedder, writing in the *Wall Street Journal* ("The Blue-State Path to Inequality", *Wall Street Journal*, June 2014) and elsewhere, point out that states like New York, Connecticut, Mississippi and California have the highest inequality, objectively measured, while states like Wyoming, Alaska, Utah and New Hampshire have the lowest. The most unequal—Washington, D.C., New York and Connecticut—are dominated by liberal policies and politics. "Four of the five states with the lowest Gini coefficients—Wyoming, Alabama, Utah and New Hampshire—are generally red states," they note. The writers concede that "our findings do not show that state redistributionist policies cause more income inequality. But they do suggest that raising tax rates or the minimum wage fail to achieve greater equality and may make income gaps wider." They go on:

> "The conclusion is nearly inescapable that liberal policy pre-scriptions—especially high income tax rates and the lack of a right-to-work law (Author's Note: Such laws prohibit non-union members from employment)—make states less prosperous because they chase away workers, businesses and capital.
>
> "Their pro-growth rivals in the South are economically bleeding northeastern states and now California to death. Toyota didn't leave California for Texas for the weather. The latest IRS report on interstate migration provides further confirmation: The states that lost the most taxpayers (as a percent of their population) were Illinois, New York, Rhode Island and New Jersey.
>
> "When politicians get fixated on closing income gaps rather than creating an overall climate conducive to prosperity, middle- and lower-income groups suffer most and income inequality rises."

As a nation, we already spend trillions of dollars redistributing income—we just don't call it that. Some of these efforts are via *means-tested* (i.e., to participate you must qualify by having a low income) efforts like food stamps (47 million recipients today—one in seven Americans—up a lot in the past six years), Medicaid and CHIPS (joint state-federal medical programs for poor adults and children, respectively, where the number of beneficiaries grew to almost 68 million in August, 2014, an increase of almost to nine million in a single year), Social Security disability (where the number of participants has grown from just over five million to almost nine million since 2000) and the Earned Income Tax Credit, an innovation enacted in 1975, modified several times thereafter, and used to good effect by President Clinton as part of his successful welfare reform effort. A host

of additional programs, though not means-tested, are quasi-redistribu-
tion programs. These include things like Social Security, unemployment,
Medicare, minimum wage, and various other subsidies. So let's understand
that there's an enormous income redistribution *already* occurring in our
country—the point that Piketty failed to acknowledge—and, importantly,
that *all these things must be paid for*.

Several questions naturally arise.

- What does this all add up to? Trillions.
- Who gets the bill? We do—the one out of two U.S. citizens who pay
  any tax—and especially the young. Mitt Romney's controversial
  assertion—for which he was pilloried—that half of Americans don't
  pay any tax was absolutely correct.
- Are they effective—i.e., do these programs relieve the distress of
  the disadvantaged? Sometimes. But they can also do great harm on
  occasion.
- Does the government run them well? Mixed results.
- Do they reduce the income inequality that so many fret about? Very
  hard to discern any gain.

Is America Being Colonized by Mexico?

The 2014 midterm election aftermath and early 2016 drumbeating
clearly signal that immigration reform will be big in the next nationwide
election. Younger voters, be prepared. Immigration has something for
everyone, so expect an almost-unprecedented level of dissembling by
all parties. At stake, you will hear, are our values (are we not a nation of
immigrants?); less often will anyone acknowledge that immigrants may
bestow 12 million new votes on the party they favor. And note the curious line-ups and associations that accompany this battle for their hearts
and minds—and recall if you can the 1969 march against farmers' use of
illegal immigrants, which featured Mexican immigrant Cesar Chavez,
with then-Senator Walter Mondale and Ralph Abernathy, president of
the Southern Christian Leadership Conference. Strange bedfellows? You
ain't seen nothing yet.

Despite consistent Republican support of reform and amnesty for
illegal aliens (mostly Mexican; some estimate that 9 percent of Mexico
lives in the U.S.), this mostly Hispanic population votes Democratic.

Not So Fast, Please

Behind the hypocrisy and demagoguery, a few distasteful facts should be noted. In recent years, Hispanics account for most of the increase in the U.S. poverty rate and Hispanic women have a high unmarried birth rate—it's three times the white rate and 1.5 times that of Black women. In recent years, most of the growth in our school population is due to Hispanic students, and by 2050, Hispanic kids are expected to comprise more than half of public school students—a huge incremental financial cost that translates directly to higher taxes.

That challenge is huge; but it's dwarfed by two other considerations—the slow rate of assimilation and high rate of incarceration (half of gang members were Hispanic/Latino in 2001).

Immigration reform is definitely not a "no-brainer"—it is serious business rich with potential both for political gain and for unintended consequences, and thus a malignant brew. We better get this one right.

Mark Levin notes in *Liberty And Tyranny*:

> "Dr. Samuel P. Huntington, who served as chairman of Harvard's Government Department and its Academy for International and Area Studies, observed that 'the persistent inflow of Hispanic immigrants threatens to divide the United States into two peoples, two cultures, and two languages. ... The United States ignores this challenge at its peril.' He argued that 'Mexican immigration differs from past immigration and most other contemporary immigration due to a combination of six factors: contiguity, scale, illegality, regional concentration (in the Southwest), persistence, and historical presence.' The consequences, he believed, are stark: 'Demographically, socially, and culturally, the Reconquista (re-conquest) of the Southwest United States by Mexican immigrants is well underway.'"

Raul Yzaguirre was for three decades president of National Council of La Raza (meaning in English, "the race") which pursued an extremely radical agenda, fought the integration of Mexicans and those who sought a common language, English, reportedly saying at one point, "U.S. English is to Hispanics as the Ku Klux Klan is to blacks." Levin reports that "Hillary Clinton appointed Yzaguirre as co-chair of her presidential campaign and assigned him to lead her outreach to Hispanics. ... President Obama appointed Cecilia Munoz, a SVP of La Raza, as director of his Office of Intergovernmental Affairs."

RACE IS NOT A BLACK AND WHITE ISSUE

The job of being a citizen is not easy. The number of issues facing young and old alike seems at times limitless. The key point is simply this—*economic issues count most* and when carefully scrutinized most other issues come down to economics or have an economic dimension—not all, but most. We help the disadvantaged most by fostering growth. And by casting a skeptical eye on all proposals from government to help them.

Racial justice is a fine example. This seems to be a straightforward case of, what is right? But over the many decades our country has struggled to achieve racial equity, economics has lurked in the weeds almost the whole time.

All of us—especially the idealistic young—are concerned about injustice—and eliminating racial injustice is close to all our hearts. No concern has sparked more government effort than those designed to redress past injustice and level the playing field for those of color.

President Lyndon Johnson's Great Society of the mid-Sixties unleashed a string of programs, including the Voting Rights Act, among others, all designed, as he said in his commencement speech at Howard University in 1965, for "the next and the more profound stage of the battle for civil rights"—"not just freedom but opportunity" and "not just equality as a right and a theory, but equality as a fact and equality as a result".

Sadly, the $20 trillion investment (in constant dollars; inclusive of all Great Society programs) has yielded few dividends—and many unintended consequences. Yes—food stamps and other elements of the safety net have tempered the human cost of the economy's ups and downs, but by several objective measures, other programs have come up short.

As Arthur Herman, a senior fellow at the Hudson Institute, noted in his February 2014 *Wall Street Journal* review of two new volumes on LBJ, "From 1959 to 1966, the number of Americans living below the poverty line had fallen to 14.7 from 22.4 percent—without the benefit of the Great Society. Since then, the poverty rate has remained stubbornly above 11 percent ... in 2012 (the year with the latest available data), it was 15 percent—slightly above the 1966 rate.

"Consider also the War on Poverty's effects, like welfare dependency. In 1983, one in five Americans belonged to a family receiving means-tested federal benefits like food stamps or Head Start (in other words, not Social Security or Medicare); in 2012 the number had risen to one in three. Family life suffered related changes, as Uncle Sam steadily replaced parents as a family's principal breadwinner and the number of reasons to remain married—or get married—dwindled away. The Great Society and the War on Poverty helped set off an explosion of out-of-wedlock births. That is one reason why the poverty rate for children today is higher than before the mid-1960s—and why more than half of black children (about whom Johnson expressed so much concern) live with their mother and why nearly half of all those children live below the poverty line."

The 1965 Voting Rights Act was the one part of the LBJ program that had powerful results—voter registration skyrocketed and the political influence of black Americans climbed significantly—after a century of contemptible, but successful efforts to block them from the voting booth. But since that positive event and the progress made in its wake, we've fumbled badly. As we commemorate the 50th anniversary of Daniel Patrick Moynihan's controversial document on the black family, issued when he was assistant secretary in Johnson's Labor Department, it is hard to discern substantive progress in the economic well-being of black Americans. In fact, in 2012, the poverty rate for all blacks was more than 28 percent.

Preserving the Liberal-Black Voting Block

The political left's serial altruism over the past half century has contributed to this. Jason Riley, black author of *Please Stop Helping Us*, asks, "have popular government policies and programs that are aimed at helping blacks worked as intended? And where black advancement has occurred, do these government efforts deserve the credit that they so often receive? The intentions behind welfare programs, for example, may be noble. But in practice they have slowed the self-development that proved necessary for other groups to advance. Minimum wage laws might lift earnings for people who are already employed, but they also have a long history of pricing blacks out of the labor force."

As Riley makes clear in his book, there is a powerful but cynical political dynamic at work here. Even though black leadership has grown increasingly unrepresentative of blacks generally, that leadership collaborates with the liberal establishment to maintain the cohesiveness of the black electorate. This has not been easy because Obama and others advocate for policies that hurt blacks. As Riley points out, "time and again, the empirical data show that current methods and approaches have come up short. Upward mobility depends on work and family. Social programs that undermine the work ethic and displace fathers keep poor people poor, and perverse incentives put in place by people trying to help are manifested in black attitudes, habits and skills."

History has confirmed the Moynihan report's emphasis that the deterioration of the black family would be aggravated and accelerated by generous government policies that penalized marriage and subsidized single parents—precisely what happened.

The tragedy of Trayvon Martin isn't quite as it seems

On February 26, 2012 George Zimmerman fatally shot Trayvon Martin in Sanford, Florida. Six weeks later, Zimmerman was charged with murder and on July 13, 2013 he was acquitted.

Al Sharpton joined Jesse Jackson, the two singled out by former Garland, Texas NAACP president C.L. Bryant as "race hustlers", in their joint pretrial determination that Martin was "murdered and martyred". Senior Fellow Shelby Steele at Stanford's Hoover Institution said that the tragedy was being exploited by a generation of "ambulance-chasing" black leaders who have promoted "our historical victimization as the central theme of our group identity."

Shelby Steele of the Hoover Institution made this observation after the verdict:

> The civil rights leadership rallied to Trayvon's cause (and not the cause of those hundreds of black kids slain in America's inner cities every year) to keep alive a certain cultural "truth" that is the sole source of the leadership's dwindling power. Put bluntly, this leadership rather easily tolerates black kids killing other black kids. But it cannot abide a white person (and Mr. Zimmerman, with his Hispanic background, was pushed into a white identity by the media over his objections) getting away with killing a black person without undermining the leadership's very reason for being.

The media frenzy shed little light on the basic facts of the event. Nor did they enlighten the general public on either Trayvon's less-than-spotless history (police had earlier found him in possession of stolen goods, but did not charge him) or Zimmerman's own Hispanic background (unmentioned by the media) or his aspirations for a law enforcement career.

A detailed reading of the case leads one to conclude that Zimmerman acted lawfully, even with courage, and that young Trayvon would, tragically, inevitably have clashed with the law—like so many of his peers.

When the jury rendered its verdict, a nationwide poll confirmed sharp divisions, with nearly 90 percent of African Americans calling the shooting unjustified (vs. 33 percent of whites), and 62 percent of Democrats vs. 20 percent of Republicans concurring. Similarly, the young found the verdict wanting—in sharp contrast of those over the age of 65.

The case illustrates every point that Jason Riley makes in his book.

> "The NAACP responded to the Zimmerman verdict by announcing a series of national legislative initiatives. Ben Jealous, the head of the group at the time, said its goal was to 'end racial profiling, repeal stand your ground laws, form effective civil complaint review boards to provide oversight of police misconduct, improve training for community watch groups, mandate law enforcement to collect data on homicide cases involving non-whites, and address the school to prison pipeline'. The NAACP, in other words, is way more interested in keeping whites on their toes than in addressing self-destructive black habits."

2014 events in Ferguson, Missouri kept these bitter issues alive. Again, the facts seem fairly straightforward: a young black man (who we now know was unarmed) robbed a store, attacked a white police officer, and was shot dead resisting arrest. And this was confirmed by a grand jury in St. Louis County that brought no charges against the officer, who subsequently resigned from the police force.

Riots, looting and mass violence then erupted. (Curiously, President Obama's response was to commission a reevaluation of the federal government's provision of surplus military weaponry to local police departments, though none of it figured in the tragic incident.)

Perhaps mercifully, Georgetown sociologist Michael Eric Dyson appears to have taken Al Sharpton's seat at this table. Writing in the *New York Times*, Dyson noted that:

"Many whites who point to blacks killing blacks are moved less by concern for black communities than by a desire to fend off criticism of unjust white cops. They have the earnest belief that they are offering new ideas to black folk about the peril we foment in our neighborhoods. ... More than 45 years ago, the Kerner Commission concluded that we still lived in two societies, one white, one black, separate and still unequal. President Lyndon B. Johnson convened that commission while the flames that engulfed my native Detroit in the riot of 1967 still burned. If our president and our nation now don't show the will and courage to speak the truth and remake the destinies of millions of beleaguered citizens, then we are doomed to watch the same sparks reignite, whenever and wherever injustice meets desperation."

—Michael Eric Dyson, "Where Do We Go After Ferguson",
New York Times, November 2014

Mr. Dyson's article was likely inspired by another, by Mr. Riley.

Referring to evidence that Michael Brown "was much more of a menace than a martyr," Riley points out that this truth didn't "stop liberals from pushing an anti-police narrative that harms the black poor in the name of helping them."

"According to the FBI, homicide is the leading cause of death among young black men, who are 10 times more likely than their white counterparts to be murdered. And while you'd never know it watching MSNBC, the police are not to blame. Blacks are just 13 percent of the population, but responsible for a majority of all murders in the U.S., and more than 90 percent of black murder victims are killed by other blacks. Liberals like to point out that most whites are killed by other whites, too. That's true but beside the point given that the white crime rate is so much lower than the black crime rate.

"Blacks commit violent crimes at seven to 10 times the rate that whites do. The fact that their victims tend to be the same race suggests that young black men in the ghetto live in danger of being shot by each other, not by cops. Nor is this a function of "over-policing" certain neighborhoods to juice black arrest rates. Research has long shown that the rate at which blacks are arrested is nearly identical to the rate at which crime victims identify blacks as their assailants. The police are in these communities because that's where the emergency calls originate, and they spend much of their time trying to stop residents of the same race from harming one another.

"And if black criminal behavior is a response to white racism, how it is that black crime rates were lower in the 1940s and 1950s, when black poverty was higher, racial discrimination was rampant and legal, and the country was more than half-century away from electing a black president?

"Racial profiling and tensions between the police and poor black communities are real problems, but these are effects rather than causes, and they can't be addressed without also addressing the extraordinarily high rates of black criminal behavior—yet such discussion remains taboo. Blacks who bring it out are sellouts. Whites who mention it are racists … so long as young black men are responsible for an outsize portion of violent crime, they will be viewed suspiciously by law enforcement and fellow citizens of all races. … But so long as young black men are responsible for an outside portion of violent crime, they will be viewed suspiciously by law enforcement and fellow citizens of all races.

"Pretending that police behavior is the root of the problem is not only a dodge but also foolish. The riots will succeed in driving business out of town, which means that Ferguson's residents will be forced to pay more at local stores or travel farther for competitive prices on basic goods and services. Many Ferguson residents today can't go to work because local businesses have been burned down.

"Even worse, when you make police targets, you make low income communities less safe. Ferguson's problem isn't white cops or white prosecutors; it's the thug behavior exhibited by individuals like Michael Brown, which puts a target on the backs of other young black men. Romanticizing such behavior instead of condemning it only makes matters worse."

—Jason L. Riley, "The Other Ferguson Tragedy", *Wall Street Journal*,
November 2014. Reprinted courtesy of the *Journal*.
Mr. Riley is a member of the *Journal's* editorial board and the author of
"Please Stop Helping Us: How Liberals Make it Harder for Blacks to Succeed"
(Encounter Books, 2014)

The Justice Department released its findings on the Ferguson developments in March 2015. These findings put the lie to the fable encouraged by an irresponsible press of what Bret Stephens calls "The double fable of 'a gentle giant' capriciously slain by a trigger-happy cop; and that a racist justice system stood behind that cop." (*Wall Street Journal*, March 2015).

The Justice Department report, according to Stephens, "demolishes the lie that he was surrendering to Mr. Wilson ... when he was shot. It confirms that Brown physically assaulted the officer, who had grounds to fear for his life. And it confirms that witnesses either lied to investigators or refused to be interviewed for fear of local vigilantes."

Crime fell in the '80s, as did incarceration rates. William Comanor and Llad Phillips looked at national longitudinal data on young people and found that "The most critical factor affecting the prospect that a male youth will encounter the criminal justice system is the presence of his father in the home." Some would say that Roe vs. Wade, which facilitated the access of poor black women to the same reproductive choice that more affluent white women had long enjoyed, meant fewer young black men raised in homes without fathers and thus less crime.

Franklin Zimring, a law professor at the University of California, Berkeley, notes with a touch of irony that: "The crime decline was the only public benefit of the 1990s whereby the poor and disadvantaged received more direct benefits than those with wealth."

The biggest single predictor that a police encounter will result in use of force by the officer is not racial bias, as many black leaders claim, but resisting arrest. And that is the circumstance that prevailed in the recent deadly events in Baltimore, Ferguson and New York's Staten Island. Those sad events fanned a powerful blowback against proactive policing methods—approaches that shrank inner city crime significantly over the past two decades—and have led to what St. Louis police chief Sam Dotson calls the "Ferguson Effect" where police are abandoning the very methods that worked so well. In New York, for example, "stop and frisk" has virtually stopped. The president and former attorney general, by appearing to embrace the lie that racism lies behind such methods, have themselves contributed to a veritable crime spree in the inner city. Across America's worst urban neighborhoods, violent crime is skyrocketing as a result of this "Ferguson Effect", with homicides, shootings, robberies, and violent felonies up dramatically in major cities.

"Contrary to the claims of the 'black lives matter' movement, no government policy in the past quarter century has done more for urban reclamation than proactive policing. Data-driven enforcement, in conjunction with stricter penalties for criminals and "broken windows" policing, brought lawful commerce and jobs to once drug-infested neighborhoods and allowed millions to go about their daily lives without fear," notes Heather MacDonald ("The New Nationwide Crime Wave", *Wall Street Journal*, May 2015).

And who is hurt most by this? You guessed it—black Americans in the inner cities.

Rev. Al Sharpton—Not So Sharp for African Americans

"Where to start in evaluating what a blessing Al Sharpton has been to New York and America? For those who have forgotten or are too young to recall, here is a brief history of the man now so warmly embraced by the mayor (Bill de Blasio, Major of New York City), the governor and the president.

"There was Mr. Sharpton's frenzied involvement in the Tawana Brawley case. In 1987 Ms. Brawley, a 15-year-old African-American, concocted a tale of being raped by six white males. The allegation was ultimately revealed as a hoax, but not before Mr. Sharpton had commandeered the racially incendiary story and poured fuel on it by accusing a white county prosecutor of having been among the attackers. The prosecutor, Steven Pagones, won a defamation suit in 1998 against Mr. Sharpton, Ms Brawley and her lawyers. Mr. Sharpton refused to pay the judgment against him, which was eventually discharged by a group of supporters.

"In 1991 a Hasidic driver in Brooklyn's Crown Heights accidentally ran onto a sidewalk and killed a 7-year-old black child named Gavin Cato. Mr. Sharpton led protestors in angry cries of 'No justice, no peace,' criticized Jewish diamond merchants in the neighborhood for selling goods from apartheid South Africa, and spoke at a rally where a banner said, 'Hitler did not do the job.' During three days of violence following the incident, rioters beat to death an Australian rabbinical student named Yankel Rosenbaum.

"In 1995 Mr. Sharpton led a protest in Harlem to stop a Jewish landlord—a 'white interloper', in Mr. Sharpton's words—from evicting a black-operated record shop. One of the protestors would later set fire to the store, killing seven store employees.

"Mr. Sharpton has never apologized for his involvement in the Brawley hoax. Nor has he taken responsibility for his agitation in Crown Heights. ...

"Despite Mr. Sharpton's current mainstream patina, his stock-in-trade has changed little from his Tawana Brawly-Crown Heights days, as the disintegration of his inflammatory narrative about the police shooting in Ferguson, Mo., demonstrates. Apart from rare forays into the rhetoric of personal responsibility, he still peddles the dangerous lie that police officers are the greatest threat facing young black men and that racial discrimination is the main force holding blacks back.

"In fact, it is other young black men who are responsible for the high homicide risk faced by black teens, and it is proactive policing that has dramatically reduced that risk, savings thousands of young lives in places like New York City."

—Heather MacDonald, "The Democratic Embrace of Al Sharpton", *Wall Street Journal*, October 2014

"(My liberal friend's) argument recalled to me Al Sharpton's championship of Tawana Brawley, whose false accusations and perjury led to the persecution of innocent police officers and the disruption of their lives. When she recanted, and admitted perjury, Reverend Sharpton suggested that though perhaps the testimony was not all it could be in this case, nevertheless, he still supported her because of the systematic history, in similar cases, of supportable claims of abuse. He was, that is, not interested in the truth."

—David Mamet, *The Secret Knowledge*

The Dark Corner in the Big Tent

Politicians of all kinds, if truly challenged (as they should be, but seldom are), would have to acknowledge the plight of young Black American men as among the biggest challenges in our society. What we see in Ferguson and Baltimore is a reflection of this much bigger problem. In a society that is riven by partisan political strife, and where single-issue 'litmus test' issues (in which they have little interest) and ideological rigidity prevail, young Black American men are the most alienated of us all. And the most disenfranchised. Their view of the world—shaped too often by poverty, by a father-less upbringing in crime-ridden, violent neighborhoods with pathetically inadequate schools which have failed them—is truly dark. So they often lack entry-level job skills, socially-acceptable role models, and any optimism about their own future. Hence, their lack of respect for authority (the police for sure, but for others as well), remarkable propensity for violence (mostly to each other) and cynicism about their country and its conventional, "white" values.

Military service has been one "out" for some of these young men. Black Americans account of 22 percent of our army and 17 percent of our armed services—and a similar proportion of those who in recent years have died for our country.

There aren't many more pathways for them to traverse.

Unless we do something, these young Black Americans represent what is truly a new Lost Generation. They are Lincoln's unfinished business.

We must make that unfinished business our own.

We have already described their erstwhile "leaders"—people like Al Sharpton. And we have noted that a symbiotic bond seems to prevail between such people and liberal politicians, who share an interest in maintaining, as they have done successfully for many decades, a coherent Black American block that votes together. And votes overwhelmingly Democratic.

Two questions logically arise.

- First, how well has this new Lost Generation of young Black Americans been served by these folks? And, most important—since the answer to the first is clearly, very badly—
- How do we build a path that enables this Lost Generation to resume the social/economic climb that Great Society and subsequent government programs so clearly interrupted?

At least four steps would help enormously.

- Improve inner city schools. Give parents a choice via vouchers and anything else that has the same effect. Don't even look twice—vote out any politician opposed to charter schools and other proven alternatives.
- Restore the full spectrum of law enforcement actions like "stop and frisk" (to which the Sharptons of the world vigorously object) that materially reduce inner city violence, most of which is directed at blacks by blacks.
- Provide meaningful subsidies that encourage employment and intact families—among them, a materially enhanced EITC.
- Ban ebonics and anything else that encourages young Black Americans to sneer at the very job and personal deportment skills necessary for them to succeed.

CHAPTER 10

Be Prepared to Get Out of Dodge

In the end, the best way to vote may be with our feet by moving
to another state—or even re-domiciling to another country—and
more of us are doing it.

You've got to know when to hold 'em, know when to fold 'em,
know when to walk away, and know when to run.

—Kenny Rogers, "The Gambler"

As we learned earlier in this book, states' efforts to reduce income inequality within their borders fail time and again, aggravating those income gaps. Yet, they persist, which leads some to the inevitable question of moving—especially to a lower tax locale since, among other things, such domiciles typically offer more employment opportunity.

Millennials and Boomers alike may face this quandary. In addition to climate, the absence of a state income or estate tax is a major reason why so many retirees desert high-tax northern states like Massachusetts and Vermont, which has the highest marginal tax rate in the country, for states like Florida.

In addition, of the 16 states that add state inheritance and estate taxes to the federal levy, both northern states have very high rates. Florida has none.

Figure 11: Three Examples of State Tax Rates

	INDIVIDUAL INCOME	SALES TAX	PROPERTY TAX (AS % OF HOUSE VALUE)
Florida	0	6.5%	.97%
Massachusetts	5.25%	6.25%	1.04%
Vermont	7.18%	6 %	1.59%

Voting With Your Feet

For a few, relinquishing their U.S. citizenship altogether in an increasingly attractive option—usually to elude the grasp of the tax collector, but sometimes out of distaste for public policy. (The U.S. is the only developed economy besides Eritrea that taxes its citizens on their worldwide income, even if they live elsewhere. The U.S. even subjects us to an exit tax should we renounce our citizenship. In 2013, 2999 individuals gave up their citizenship or green cards, up from 1,781 in 2011. A record 1,335 renounced their U.S. citizenship or long-term residency in 2015's first quarter. Observers ascribe the rise to that need to file, as all U.S. citizens are obliged to do, despite living offshore for decades (the IRS is after offshore bank accounts), and the large penalties to those who fail to do so. (IRS Commissioner John Koskinen reported early in 2014 that more than 43,000 U.S. taxpayers have since 2009 availed themselves of a special program for those with undeclared offshore accounts; they've paid more than $6 billion in back taxes, interest and penalties.)

Many foreign nations are making it more attractive for those with assets to move, often without relinquishing U.S. citizenship. Typically linking temporary or permanent residency to investment, this isn't cheap. Former British colony and EU member Malta, for example, will make you a full citizen in a year with a $1.25 million property investment—and allow you to retain your U.S. passport. Malta received more than 400 "naturalization" applications last year; clearly, the concept of citizenship is changing in some quarters.

You Can't Make This Stuff Up

Expats may be subject to an exit tax—which recalls the ruse played by John McClaughry, founder of Vermont's free market Ethan Allen Institute think tank. Serving in the state senate in 1991, when the governor promoted a bill dramatically jacking up the top three income tax brackets. McClaughry drafted a phony amendment labeled "Exit Tax", to be levied at the same percentage rates on the departee's net worth as the governor's legislation. He thoughtfully added a provision authorizing the Governor to call up the National Guard to collect the tax due if necessary. When word leaked, as he'd intended all along, one very liberal Democratic senator offered to co-sponsor the legislation—until realizing she had been had.

Just Follow the U-Hauls

An Inquiry into the Nature and Causes of the Wealth of States: How Taxes, Energy, and Worker Freedom Change Everything (Arthur Laffer & various co-authors, including Stephen Moore; published by John Wiley & Sons) reports a simple result. High taxation is a high motivator. People will move to avoid taxation.

"Taxation doesn't generate revenue, it moves people," Laffer says any chance he gets. It even moved Laffer, a devoted, if frustrated Californian for many years. In 2007, he took up residence in Tennessee, one of the nine states that has no state tax on 'earned' income. (Only seven states have no income tax at all; Tennessee and New Hampshire tax investment income.)

According to Laffer's worth-visiting website, which compares the individual states, a couple with $300,000 gross income from wages and salaries would save more than $17,000 a year by moving and avoiding the California income tax. Even if such a couple had $70,000 in interest, dividends, and capital gains, they would save more than $10,000 a year. You can easily estimate the potential saving of moving to another state at www.savetaxesbymoving.com.

Travis Brown, one of Laffer's co-authors, draws a map on his website (www.howmoneywalks.com) using IRS data that show, state by state and county by county, how much adjusted gross income grows legs and walks away. It also shows where the money goes.

Another story is the corporate version of this—"inversions", where a U.S.-domiciled corporation enters into a merger or other transaction with another firm in a lower tax country and takes the foreign address as their tax domicile. Highly controversial, and bitterly opposed by the Obama administration, others merely see it as a rational response to the U.S.

corporate tax regime—at 35 percent the highest in the developed world. (Though, it should be noted, many corporations pay considerably less. Companies can offset taxes with depreciation and other non-cash charges, reducing their reported tax bills, which nevertheless remain comparatively high. Corporations' contribution to overall federal tax revenue has been quite stable at about 20 percent for several years.) It can also free up some of the Bloomberg-estimated $2 trillion in U.S. companies' cash sitting offshore for reluctance to pay the "toll gate" charge to bring it home.

Figure 12: High Corporate Taxes Make the U.S. Uncompetitive

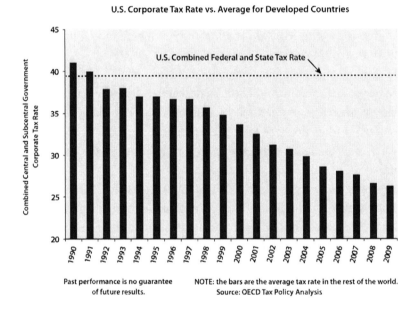

U.S. Corporate Tax Rate vs. Average for Developed Countries

Past performance is no guarantee of future results.

NOTE: the bars are the average tax rate in the rest of the world. Source: OECD Tax Policy Analysis

There have been 20 inversions since 2004, not counting sectors like the Bermuda-based insurance companies. Medtronic—the maker of cardiac arrhythmia devices—is just one recent example of a growing trend started by notorious miscreant Tyco International Ltd.

Recently joining Medtronic at the exit: pharma giant Pfizer.

CHAPTER 11

What the Young Must Do to Build Their Net Worth

Two things. Take care of business—your personal financial life, including work, savings, investing, planning for the future. Here's some practical, state-of-the-art advice about improving your economic well-being, short- and long-term. Second, you've got to step up and embrace change—that most difficult of all things. New government practices start with each of us and it won't happen without all of us.

Okay, okay. Enough already. I HEAR you, Millennial. "Those bastards in Washington, along with my parents, have put me behind the eight ball. The folks are going to die broke in Wrinkle City, Florida and those thieving guys in DC will be living in the South of France on MY tax dollars."

What can I do? Or is it simply too late? Can I still build a decent nest egg?

In reverse order, the answers are, "yes", "no" and "a lot."

There's a lot that you MUST do. Let's take these things in declining order of significance and ease of doing. And bear in mind—although you've suffered at our hands financially, you retain a powerful asset that we Boomers lack—time. It's on your side.

First, make sure your parents have a good estate plan. Offer to pay for it, if you must. An estimated one of every two Americans die without such a plan, leaving billions to the government that could have been earmarked for their children or others. There is simply no reason for them to hand over to the Feds money that could be yours. Sure—this may not be a comfortable conversation, but you've got to have it—the sooner the better.

'Do as We Do, Not as We Would Have You Do'

Bill and Hillary Clinton and have supported higher estate taxes for some time, and the centerpiece of Hillary's campaign is reversing income inequality by taxing the rich at much higher levels. In his last campaign, the former president proposed to cap the per-person exemption at $3.5 million and set the top rate at 45 percent. Without such a levy, he argued, the U.S. could become "dominated by inherited wealth."

The Clintons, by Hillary's report, left the White House "dead broke" (a claim many have contested), but have certainly prospered since—combine speeches at up to $700,000 a pop and the joys of compounding and some estimate the couple's net worth today at more than $200 million.

To reduce their (and—on their demise—Chelsea's) tax bill, they have set up residence trusts, which means that any increase in the value of their real estate happens outside their estate (and thus doesn't count in the cap, after which high taxes are assessed). We may reliably assume they are using other techniques as well.

You—and your parents—should, too.

This issue of tax-avoiding financial strategies—used to withering effect against Mitt Romney in 2012—would, in light of the Clintons' public record, make an interesting debate question in the upcoming election.

Sowell on 'Greed'

"Among the many other questions raised by the nebulous concept of 'greed' is why it is a term applied almost exclusively to those who want to earn more money or to keep what they have already earned—never to those wanting to take other people's money in taxes or to those wishing to live on the largess dispensed from such taxation. No amount of taxation is ever described by the anointed as 'greed' on the part of government or the clientele of government. ...

"Families who wish to be independent financially and to make their own decisions about their lives are of little interest or use to those who are seeking to impose their superior wisdom and virtue on other people. Earning their own money makes these families unlikely candidates for third-party direction or wishing to retain what they have earned threatens to deprive the anointed of the money needed to distribute as largess to others who would thus become subject to their direction. In these circumstances, it is understandable why the desire to increase and retain one's own earnings should be characterized negatively as 'greed', while wishing to live at the expense of others is not."

—Thomas Sowell, *The Vision of the Anointed*

Keep working. Sorry—there's no way around that. Furthermore, assume you will keep working—longer in fact than your parents probably and likely until you're at least 70. Retirement at 65 or younger is a thing of the past. (Look at the good news—if you're 35, your life expectancy is more than 80 years!) For this reason, if no other, try to involve yourself in work you truly enjoy. Also, and very importantly, try if you can to work in a tax-efficient way. What do we mean by that? Simply this—work in a way that minimizes your taxes. For example, an entrepreneur might offer you stock in lieu of cash; if you believe in the project, opt for the equity interest. Or, perhaps your employer offers to pay you in goods and services, say a leased vehicle, rather than cash—if it makes sense, do it. Don't neglect the tax advantages of work that involves cash compensation—waiting on tables, for example. Yes, we do hear that the government is "clamping down" on "unreported income", but there is still plenty of opportunity to put the tax-free cash in your pocket. And trust us—the remarkable level of tax compliance we've had in the U.S. to date is about to decline significantly as the tax burden climbs. After all, this is why they had that Tea Party in Boston Harbor so many years ago. Do whatever you can to minimize reported income.

Save. The recent recession sparked an ephemeral boost in Millennial savings rates—to almost 6 percent briefly in 2009—but, punished by the weak job market for their skills (unemployment for under-35-year-olds is now more than 6 percent and 20 percent for those 20-24) and their student loan burden, it's now a -2 percent, meaning you're eating into what savings you may have put aside and increasing your debt (typically high rate credit card debt). This leaves the young increasingly without a buffer or safety net. For those with some money in the bank, short-term rates are very low, and the savings don't throw off much return these days, at least if invested conventionally. No matter—saving should be second nature to you; if it isn't, make it so.

Keep more. Be tax smart about how you save. For example, everyone should have an IRA, preferably (generally) a Roth IRA. Participate in your employer retirement plan so as to get 100 percent matching. Contribute the maximum allowed ($18,000 in 2015, plus $6,000 if you're over the age of 50). IRA plans (be aware that, like that "limited time only free offer", restrictions do apply) allow you to put away up to $5,500 each year (plus another $1,000 for those age 50 or older; note that the self-employed can contribute a lot more—up to $52,000 a year!). Limits for 401(k) plans are much more generous—permitting up to $17,500 of pretax income to be contributed each year, with those 50 years old or more allowed another $5,000. In both IRAs and 401(k)'s, the money is yours forever; unlike Social Security, they can't take it away from you or modify its terms. (Beware: In 2013, Obama proposed that new contributions to these tax-advantaged plans be stopped once combined account balances hit $3.2 million. Fortunately, this concept stalled in Congress. There was also discussion in Washington of the government expropriating private IRA balances of more than $1 million, their assumption being "who needs more?".) And, in the end, you can bequeath what's left to your own children or others. Your investment gains grow tax-free and, in the case of a Roth, principal can be withdrawn tax-free regardless of how much of that principal represents investment gains. There is no reason not to start with a 401(k), then later convert it to an IRA plan.

There are ways to significantly augment such plans. You can contribute low cost-basis stock from a start-up, for example, as some Silicon Valley entrepeneurs have done, effectively shielding them from tax on outsized gains when their firms prosper or go public; this works just as well for small companies, too, and is how Mitt Romney managed to build a plan balance of more than $100 million.

In his 2015 State of the Union speech, President Obama conceded that private savings plans like these are important and authorized the Treasury to offer a new type of Roth IRA to those without access to a (401)K or other company-sponsored plan. He called in a "myRA" (for "my retirement account"). Free to open and fundable with as little as $25, individuals making less than $129,000 and couples making less than $191,000 would be able to open and, when the balance reaches $15,000, convert to a Roth IRA at any sponsoring firm. Expected launch—sometime in 2015.

CANADA: A BETTER WAY

In the U.S., about 31 percent of us have set up IRAs since they were authorized in 1974 as part of ERISA (Employee Retirement Income Security Act), enacted under President Gerald R. Ford. Total assets in IRA's are now $7 trillion. In contrast, 48 percent of our neighbors to the north have set up what they call TFSAs (short for "Tax-free Savings Accounts") and they accounted for $109 billion in assets at 2013 yearend.

Unlike a U.S. Roth, TFSAs have no limit on income ($191,000 joint in the U.S.), more generous contribution limits (up to $5,500 a year, like ours, but you can "make up" one year's shortfall the next without penalty) and withdrawal rights (okay tax-free at any time, unlike here, where penalties are assessed for premature withdrawal).

Writing in the *Wall Street Journal*, Amity Schlaes, board chair at the Calvin Coolidge Presidential Foundation, and Chris Edwards, director of tax policy at the Cato Institute, say, "the U.S. is primed for its own TFSA. ... Creating such an account would not be difficult for lawmakers, certainly not compared with revamping the whole tax system. Congress can simply expand eligibility and lift limits on the Roth IRA format. ... We believe this new vehicle—call it the Universal Savings Account—would be so attractive that Americans' would select it over education savings accounts or traditional programs, especially if its annual contribution limit is $7,000 or $8,000."

Set up a Health Savings Account. We can argue about what ails the U.S. healthcare system (as we do earlier) and we can speculate about the fate of Obamacare. What's important right now is building assets—assets that YOU control, not the government, while providing for both your immediate and future needs. HSAs directly address the single biggest reason our healthcare costs have mushroomed out of control. They do something quite remarkable: they put the power of the checkbook back in the hands of the consumer.

Typically combined with a low premium, high-deductible catastrophe policy that protects you from the costs associated with a serious disease like cancer, or a chronic one like diabetes, you contribute every year to an HSA and enjoy considerable freedom as to how you spend the money as long as it's for approved healthcare-related (e.g., chiropractic, massage, eye care, dental, even acupuncture).

A HSA lets you put away $3,300 a year ($6,500 for a family and an extra $1,000 if you're 55 or older)—and it's "triple tax-free" because you put in pretax income and it grows tax-free and there's no tax when you take it out (for health-related bills), unlike an IRA withdrawal. For this reason, once you've contributed as much as possible to your 401(K) or IRA, it makes sense to contribute the maximum to your HSA—in effect, treating it as a second IRA.

Some have estimated that a young married couple that enjoy typical health over their lives, with average mortality and morbidity, can accumulate up to $245,000 in such a plan by the time they reach 65. And it's their money—every step of the way. You are even free to bequeath the outstanding balance on your untimely demise.

Build a healthy lifestyle. Do that and you will live a very long time. Don't smoke. Drink in moderation. Exercise. Eat right. Get check-ups. In a few years, you can add another—have your genetic makeup profiled— but, not quite yet.

Invest intelligently. Ah, you're thinking, there's the rub. How DOES one invest intelligently? Your peers (and your parents) are asking themselves the same question. Decimated in 2008 when the financial crisis hit, the young and old have stayed out of the stock market; meanwhile, it's tripled off the bottom, reached in March 2009. It didn't matter what you owned—you made a lot of money. You just had to be there. And likely, you weren't. This risk-aversion has ample precedent in our history—one reason that retail investing activity is seen by the pros as a reliable "inverse" indicator of the stock market outlook. And it is a major factor behind the financial inequality being debated today.

As reported in the *Wall Street Journal* ("Market Missteps Fuel Inequality", Josh Zumbrun, October 2014), University of Michigan researchers Bing Chen and Frank Stafford, find that the households with the highest education and portfolios at the beginning of the recession were more likely to keep buying stocks during the decline; those with less education and smaller brokerage accounts were more likely to sell into the decline. This again proved costly. As Zumbrun points out, "Imagine two households, each with $100,000 in the stock market in 2007. A family that sold in 2009 after losing half its portfolio's value may now have $50,000 in a savings account. A family that held on would now have about $130,000 in stocks."

FAMA ON EXCHANGE-TRADED FUNDS ('ETFs')

Nobel Prize winner Eugene Fama, professor at the Booth School of Business, University of Chicago, is well known for his contribution to the theory that stock prices reflect all that we can legally (i.e., without insider trading) know about individual stocks. He also, working with others, has found that certain other factors, like smaller, low-P/E stocks, can sometimes provide above-average returns. These factors lead some ETF producers to offer special ETFs "tweaked" to reflect these distinctions. Interviewed before a packed conference hall at a 2013 Morningstar conference, Barron's shared this exchange between Fama and the moderator:

> *On when active management makes sense:* "When is it good? The answer is never. That's a really difficult perspective to get people to accept."
>
> *On why people keep investing with active managers:* "Why? I don't know. The individual is clearly so much better off (in index products). It's laughable."
>
> *On how many actively managed mutual funds beat their benchmark:* "Before costs, about 50 percent beat the index. But that's exactly what you'd expect by chance. You can't tell luck from skill."

There are a few things you should know about investing that your broker probably has never told you.
- Simple math tells us that it's impossible for active investors, on average, to outperform a passive index fund, after fees and expenses. The recent evidence once again confirms the (expensive) mediocrity of active managers. In late 2014, the margin of underperformance was the worst in almost two decades with little more than 90 percent of big cap managers lagging the S & P 500.

- Retail investors typically buy those investments—stocks or mutual funds—that have already done well. Sadly, "chasing performance" rarely works because superior performance very seldom persists. The term is "mean reversion."
- Brokers and other intermediaries don't get paid based on YOUR performance. Hedge funds do—but take an egregiously high percentage of your gains (typically, 2 percent of the assets under management annually plus 20 percent of any gains you make—of which there have been few of late). There's a reason I initially named my hedge fund FRIWAFT Partners—for "Fools Rush In Where Angels Fear to Tread".
- Most active hedge fund managers seldom outperform over time.

The reason for all this mediocrity is paradoxical—because so many investors are so smart, so well paid and incentivized, and so well supported by their employers, it's virtually impossible to beat them all with any consistency. They collectively make the market "efficient" (as the scholars say), meaning that everything that is legally knowable about stocks is already in their prices. Bernie Madoff took a different approach, Ivan Boesky yet another.

This body of knowledge—trust me, the finance literature is large and meticulously done, but no one has to date convincingly challenged market efficiency—has spawned one of the best new ideas in investing—the rise of the ETF, or Exchange Traded Fund. In their simplest forms, these are "mini index funds" designed to mimic some objective benchmark, like the S & P 500. Their fees are very low, their strategies are clearly expressed and their portfolios automatically updated. They do many really good things for you:

- They cut your costs.
- They are tax-efficient.
- They provide all the diversity you might desire.
- They enable you to skirt silly rules, like the prohibition against using margin in a pension account (like your IRA), which you can do by using leveraged ETFs.
- They facilitate your use of leverage and enable you to customize it to your risk preferences.
- There are almost 6,000 of them, a number that grows all the time (even though some close for lack of investor interest), with total assets of almost $3 trillion, affording you tremendous choice in

designing a portfolio. And they are truly global—in fact, they are growing even more rapidly in Asia than the U.S.

Any good online broker like Schwab offers excellent search engines that enable you to screen this and other investing universes and to assess relative performance and expense. You should put your account with such a broker (which Barron's periodically evaluates and ranks by several meaningful standards).

The writer has found over many decades (and, yes, I do consistently outperform the indexes) that a few considerations can tangibly enhance your investing success.

The key to outperforming all those really smart professional managers is to bet against them. And in this, you have a very strong ally—call it institutional constraints. Most investment advisors have a simple priority—keep the customers' money; this means that they are reluctant to take outsize risk because if they bet wrong you take your money elsewhere. Their primary incentive is to hold onto your money and it's often stronger than the desire to achieve great results for you. In the case of mutual funds, it means that fund boards, when they evaluate the managers' performance, look at how closely the funds followed the charter spelled out in the prospectus, which almost always leads them to ask, *how closely did the fund track the relevant index?* To which I reply, then why not buy the index (i.e., the ETF)?

So my first suggestion is—and this is totally compatible with the body of knowledge mentioned earlier—if you want to outperform, systematically deviate from those benchmarks.

As an example, one way to do this is to favor low beta (i.e., less volatile) stocks that trade at cheap valuations, have begun to show some momentum, earnings growth and where the insiders are buying in size. That's a real sweet spot. But, who knows how long it will last?

CALLING MARKET TURNS: WHAT YOUR INVESTMENT ADVISOR PROBABLY DOES NOT EVEN KNOW

Markets are complex adaptive systems (CASs)—one reason why, to make sense of them, requires more than a financial/investment background, but also some familiarity with politics (What will Washington do?), psychology (Is this spike reality-based or emotional?), and history

(Is it a reliable guide to what's going on now?), for starters.

We are still wondering, for example, what REALLY happened on Black Monday, October 19, 1987 when the Dow Jones Industrial Average crashed 508 points or almost 23 percent—or in 1929, for that matter. And for good reason, because there has been no clear cut identifiable reason we could point to.

CASs are systems with many interacting participants who learn—from their experience and from each other—and adapt. Markets of all kinds anywhere are good examples. In contrast to the canon of efficient markets (i.e., all that is legally knowable is in prices), the new Fractal Market Hypothesis challenges the Efficient Market Hypothesis assumption that all markets participants have the same time horizon.

Because in fact they don't.

These participants range from high frequency traders for whom a split second can be a lifetime and who therefore pay millions to access the record of trading first, to Warren Buffet, whose investment horizon is indeed a lifetime.

These different investors buy and sell for different reasons and their equally varied time horizons optimize market liquidity—the ability to buy and sell without inducing price change. When one group of market participants, and their time horizon, comes to dominate, even by withdrawing from the market, liquidity breaks down. Put another way, the market's "fractal dimension" breaks down. And that induces significant price change.

What's important is this—we can measure that fractal structure and hence foresee major turning points in markets—any markets. This happens when the fractal dimension approaches 1.25—and this finding holds up across asset classes, geography and generations.

For more, read *Fractal Market Analysis* (Wiley) and/or *The (Mis) Behavior Of Markets—A Fractal View Of Financial Turbulence* by Benoit Mandelbrot and Richard L. Hudson.

Note also that The Bank Credit Analyst organization, Montreal, Canada, has recently introduced a unique research product that offers trading advice based on fractals and fractal indices. Who knows what we'll learn as their record unfolds, but it will be interesting to see if this turns out to be a truly new approach to the challenge of investing successfully.

Where are Prices Going?

The inflation/deflation question is probably the most important question we all will face over the next few years and the most important determinant of how well we will fare as we seek to build our net worth.

Inflation destroys the value of assets as it lowers the value of debt—one reason governments always resort to this way of lowering the real costs of their accumulated debt. Deflation, on the other hand (there's the economist's favorite expression again), encourages people to defer spending as declining prices lower the price of the goods and services they might wish to buy. But, this in turn depresses overall demand, causing growth to abate even faster, and investment to decline as well.

Inflation benefits the debtor (like Uncle Sam), deflation the saver (his bucks buy more and more).

As we write this, the central banks of the developed world (and many others as well) are more worried about deflation. This fear has been aggravated recently by the abrupt and significant decline in energy prices. Some speculate that central bankers' fear of deflation is almost paralyzing (Mario Draghi, leader of the ECB, has clearly struggled to build support in Europe for more aggressive steps to rekindling growth and inflation, like Quantitative Easing).

It was this fear that led Ben Bernanke to say, in answer to a question about how he'd deal with deflation, that he'd drop dollar bills out of airplanes (hence the sobriquet "Helicopter Ben"). A student of the Depression, Bernanke has traced how the Smoot-Hawley Tariff depressed global trade, causing worldwide economic contraction as a result; the Fed then shrank the monetary base in response to a declining economy thereby aggravating and prolonging the economic suffering into WWII—a classic and riveting case of central bank policy failure.

What does this mean to you? Possibly a lot. Whether we are in or headed into an inflationary or deflationary period matters profoundly to your financial and investment planning.

So Where DID That Bastard Come From?

Prices shape history. Casual readers of history commonly associate the rise of Hitler and the Nazis with the hyperinflation of the Weimar Republic, when the German mark (their pre-Euro currency)-to-dollar exchange rate went from 4.2-to-1 in 1914 to 4.2 million-to-1 in 1923! As you'd expect, these exploding prices traumatized some (savers), but provided relief to others (debtors). Today, Draghi's efforts to get the European economy moving have been impeded by Germany's continuing concern about a recurrence.

In fact, however, the Nazi's rise to power was driven much more by the deflation that came after Chancellor Bruning sought to stem a government deficit and gold outflows in 1930 with deflation policies which killed the economy and hurt everyone. They set off a powerfully self-enforcing negative feedback loop which produced an eager and desperate audience for Hitler's promises of stable prices and rising employment.

We've seen prices move in both directions in recent years, but with the exception of the '70s, these changes have been mild. Then, the prime rate—the interest rate banks charge their best customers, reached 22 percent as Paul Volcker, Fed head, wrestled a 15 percent annual inflation rate to the ground.

Fortunately, Volcker's harsh antidote to the "guns and butter" spending of the Johnson years curtailed the resulting inflation. But, it was painful and occasionally scary. Few can forget Henry Kissinger's somber warning at the time: "Double digit interest rates are incompatible with democracy."

The recent housing debacle reminds us that you don't want to have a lot of debt when the price of the associated asset goes down (i.e., deflates). Interestingly, the stock market has performed better during deflationary periods than during periods of high inflation—a likely reason being that markets were recovering after economic slowdown induced the Fed to cut rates; 2009 is a good example, but there've been three other episodes since 1940. Taking a longer-term horizon, there've been several episodes of inflation and deflation. The investment implication this history presents is simply this: if modest (limited to 2 percent or less either way), stocks do well. Exceed that band, however, and better watch out.

This is confirmed by the derivatives markets where products called inflation "caps" and "floors" foretell investors' expectations of future prices. In the spring of 2015 they implied that it was twice as likely that inflation will come in below the Fed's 2 percent target as not. But, stay tuned.

Today, inflation looks to be a distant threat. There is a global savings glut. In China, for example, the difference between savings and investment is 10 percent of their GDP or more than $1.1 trillion. Such money must find a home.

When inflation draws closer (not "if", "when"), you want to own stocks, commodities and the like—risk assets. Favor technology stocks (or technology ETFs), in my view, under both inflationary and deflationary scenarios because these companies know how to live with both—their product/service prices already decline all the time, but they know how to adapt, and when we inflate, companies will substitute capital (i.e., technology) for more expensive labor.

Be informed. Finally, the most important thing you must do to build your net worth as tax-efficiently as possible is to be better informed than everyone else who's trying to do the same thing. That's tough. Of course, with smart public and tax policies, this is far better than a zero sum game—everyone CAN win—but it will take a while to turn our national drift around; until that happens, wealth creation faces many challenges. Some of them are informational. And the most important information for us is often remote.

Think of those two economic expressions mentioned earlier—"search costs" and "information asymmetry." Joseph Stiglitz, a liberal economist, got the Nobel in Economics for his work on the latter. Again, these terms simply refer to how disparate or symmetric information sets (for example, your knowledge of attractive investments compared to that of a partner at Goldman Sachs) are—perfectly overlapping vs. widely different, and how hard it is for us to achieve congruence.

Here are some suggestions on how to do so.

Read the *Wall Street Journal* every day. Stephen Moore says that this newspaper is unique in that "It prints the news on the editorial page and the speculation on the news page." I agree. In this writer's view, there's more intellectual integrity and solid information in the *Journal* than any other publication in the U.S. (maybe anywhere). And you can read it every day except Sunday!

I had the pleasure many years ago of meeting both the late, great Louis Rukeyser, the pioneer of TV financial journalism, and his remarkable mother, a fabulously talented poet; Lou single-handedly did more to fulfill Lord Keynes entreaty ("The world needs more economists") with his show on PBS, *Wall Street Week*, than anyone else. Today, we have several financial broadcasts that offer superb access to really good information and perspective on the economy and markets. Don't miss CNBC and Neil

Cavuto, Larry Kudlow and John Stossel—terrific commentators all. The best journalists in America work on these shows and they provide daily access to the best minds around.

And when you have an idle moment, let me suggest that you Google folks like those described below.

- Financial scholars are always worth reading and several come to mind—Yale's Robert Shiller, Princeton's Burton Malkiel, Chicago's Richard Thaler, and many others.
- Gretchen Morgenson's Sunday *New York Times* column "Fair Game" is unrivaled in how it illuminates darker corners of the business world and Wall Street.
- My friend Joel Stern pioneered the study of how companies build shareholder value (as did I, for that matter) and contributed greatly to our knowledge of this process. Google him.
- Jack Treynor, formerly editor of the then-*Financial Analysts Journal* (now the *Journal of Investment Management*). Jack should get a Nobel for his work, in the view of Richard Brealey, formerly London Business School dean.
- Charlie Ellis, founder of Greenwich Research Associates, writes with great insight—his *Loser's Game* is a classic on successful investing.
- Adam Smith's *The Money Game* remains a riveting read.
- Berkshire Hathaway's annual report, with its shareholder message from Warren Buffet, is "a must read." Toronto-based Fairfax Financial isn't far behind.

The list is long and growing—as it should for the markets are where everything comes together.

Read voraciously. See the bibliography at the back of this book for some top-notch reads. After you've bought a couple of books on these financial subjects through Amazon, they will alert you to new offerings.

The great thing about being a purposive investor is that you will never stop learning, And, as race car driver Dan Gurney once said of coming into a 30 MPH curve at 130 MPH, your reading—like his brakes—"will assume a very personal meaning."

CHAPTER 12

We CAN Believe in America Again

Sometimes we need a breakdown to get a breakthrough—and we may get one. There is a malignancy in America. We see its early signs in diminishing tax compliance and growth of the underground, cash-based economy. We can restore America's promise— by joining Millennials and Boomers, Democrats, Republicans, Libertarians, on the middle ground. We can restore the dream we shared for two centuries.

There are few things more chilling than a diagnosis of cancer. I know. I've had four different kinds.

Bad as that initial news may be, so too is the tension that builds inexorably as one goes through various diagnostic tests so that the cancer may "staged"—that is, its gravity (and your chances of survival) may be estimated and appropriate treatment prescribed.

The only thing that is worse is a tardy diagnosis, for the longer cancer goes undetected, the more the odds of survival decline.

There is a malignancy growing in America and, like a cancer, it has flourished as we've ignored the early warning signs. Those signs included a continuing tolerance for:

- Wasteful government programs that fail,
- Regulations that shackle American entrepreneurs and disadvantage them versus their offshore rivals,

- The unintended consequences of government actions with paradoxical and costly outcomes,
- Foreign adventures that end badly and usurp funding for worthy domestic efforts, like broader healthcare coverage.
- Rising government debt, most of it not honestly accounted for.
- Government ineptitude at virtually every level, as officials stray far from their legitimate tasks.
- But, above all, we've drawn further and further apart, with little agreement on how to solve our country's ills.

Time and again, our country has come together to solve great challenges. The fuel that enabled us to win two world wars, dominate space, lead the world in technology of all kinds and, consistently for two centuries—until now—raise the well-being of successive generations is optimism, faith in the future.

But today, signs abound that we are losing faith in the future, in ourselves, and in the exceptionalism that some deny but which indelibly marks American history. This loss reflects itself in our growing distaste with Washington, with government at all levels, even with each other as we quarrel amongst ourselves about issues far removed from our gravest ills.

Look at the attitudes of you and your friends—don't you, too, sense a growing hopelessness? What will ever change? has become a too-common refrain.

This malignancy often becomingly cloaks itself in concern for the disadvantaged—the "narcissistic altruism" mentioned earlier, sometimes in combative stands on issues of little enduring relevance that merely affirm our status as good "virtucrats." And sometimes it seeks comfort from old, false truths like "creationism" or "marriage is only between a man and woman." Whatever form it takes, its concealment diverts us away from the central issue—rekindling economic growth and increasing prosperity in which all may share—and from our core values of tolerance, freedom, individualism. And it complicates the acknowledgment and diagnosis of our ills all the while.

Now, we find our country somewhere between "Stage 3" (we've got a chance) and "Stage 4" (we better be sure our affairs are in order).

It IS different this time.

We don't have any more wiggle room.

Like the grim choice many cancer patients may face—between do nothing (our choice to date as citizens), surgery, chemotherapy, radiation, or all three—this medicine also takes several forms, all unpleasant.

- We've got to cut government spending, which means fewer goodies from Uncle Sam. For us and everyone else. Let's not forget—each of us is a "special interest", too.
- We must change how we fund the spending that remains and, to do that, we must do two things:
- Accelerate our ability to force change—e.g., by putting in term limits and requiring that retiring congressmen and senators be prohibited from anything like lobbying their former colleagues (as 400 of them do today), and—by shutting down stupid government programs and their too-often unintended consequences. We need to celebrate the END of government programs the way we used to celebrate their start. And, need we add, the politicians who enacted them.
- Finally, *we ourselves must change.*
- And we must be merciless—or we will die in an America we never envisioned that is bleak, broke and bereft of promise.

Let's take the toughest one. How must we change?

We must rekindle civic pride. We have to know the key issues and think about them clearly and objectively. Economic growth. Less regulation. A cleaner tax code. No fraud. Healthcare for all in a system that works.

Serious fiscal issues in themselves threaten to tear us apart, so can't we set aside so-called "wedge" issues—the ones that may appear to say something about our values or our identity, but don't solve the big problem?

A good example is choice.

Choice is a litmus issue for most women—my wife's bumper sticker says, "If you can't trust me with a choice, how can you trust me with a child?"—and understandably; it's your bodies we're talking about. A wise person said, if men could get pregnant, choice would be in the Bill of Rights.

Oppose choice, and in a run-off against Quasimoto, you would lose. Fact is, however, that there is zero chance that access to reproductive rights will be outlawed in the U.S. Zero. Yes, it's conceivable that it might get banned in some state until an appeal wound its way to the Supreme Court. But for the vast majority of women (and men) in America this simply isn't up for debate anymore.

Another is the minimum or "living" wage." We've already cited some objective research on this issue. It shows that raising minimum wage rates thwarts access by the most needy to job opportunity. However you come out after reading that analysis, can we agree that it pales in comparison to the much, much larger challenges of dealing with the family breakdown, high crime rate, and substandard schools that do so much to fan the anger we see in Ferguson and Baltimore?

Replace the Minimum Wage With a Better EITC

Across the U.S., the minimum wage is being raised—to as high as $15 an hour. But look closer and you find that such steps are just more examples of officials forsaking objective, analytical thinking (the kind that leads to solving problems, rather than coating them with misspent tax dollars) with designed-to-make-you-and-me-feel-good-about-ourselves "virtocracy."

There is a better way—the earned income tax credit ("EITC") and its record in shrinking inequality and cutting poverty (by millions of people) while lifting more children out of poverty (a quarter) than all other entitlement programs. All of this in stark contrast to the minimum wage.

Enacted in 1975 during the Ford administration, it's been affirmed by both Republican and Democratic presidents. Other entities—almost 30 states and some municipalities—have also introduced a version of the tax credit.

Payments of the EITC to workers diminish as their incomes increase, but in such a way that the incentive to work remains—more wages always means more total income.

Those incentives work! They account for half the rise in the number of single mothers who work, as one example.

The EITC helps assure that benefits of economic growth are shared by all—what should be the central theme today in our public policy debate.

Billionaire investor Warren Buffet recently noted ("Better than Raising the Minimum Wage", *Wall Street Journal*, May 22, 2015) that, compared to minimum wage boosts, "The better answer is a major and carefully crafted expansion of the (EITC), which currently goes to millions of low-income workers. ... The existing EITC needs much improvement. Fraud is a big problem (Author's Note: before recent changes, fraud was once a fifth of total spending.): penalties for it should be stiffened. There should be widespread publicity that workers can receive free and convenient filing help. An annual payment is now the rule; monthly installments would make more sense, since they would discourage people from taking out loans while waiting for their refunds to come through. Dollar amounts should be increased, particularly for those earning the least."

Figure 13: Working-Family Tax Credits Help at Every Stage of Life

The Earned Income Tax Credit (EITC) and Child Tax Credit (CTC) not only reward work and reduce poverty for low- and moderate-income working families with children, but a growing body of research shows that they help families at virtually every stage of life:

Improved infant and maternal health: Researchers have found links between increased EITCs and improvements in infant health indicators such as birth weight and premature birth. Research also suggests receiving an expanded EITC may improve maternal health.

Better school performance: Elementary and middle-school students whose families receive larger refundable credits (such as the EITC and CTC) tend to have higher test scores in the year of receipt.

Greater college enrollment: Young children in low-income families that benefit from expanded state or federal EITCs are more likely to go to college, research finds. Researchers attribute this to lasting academic gains from higher EITCs in middle school and earlier. Increased tax refunds also boost college attendance by making college more affordable for families with high-school seniors, research finds.

Increased work and earnings in the next generation: For each $3,000 a year in added income that children in a working-poor family receive before age 6, they work an average of 135 more hours a year between ages 25 and 37 and their average annual earnings increase by 17 percent, leading researchers have found.

Social Security retirement benefits: Research suggests that by boosting the employment and earnings of working-age women, the EITC boosts their Social Security retirement benefits, which should reduce poverty in old age. (Social Security benefits are based on how much one works and earns.)

Note: For further details on the research see Chuck Marr, Chye-Ching Huang, and Arloc Sherman, "Earned Income Tax Credit Promotes Work, Encourages Children's Success at School, Research Finds," CBPP

School choice. Let's acknowledge the evidence—teachers' unions work for teachers, not students, and therefore oppose choice, vouchers and the charter schools that are proving to be highly effective, especially for young Black American children who would otherwise suffer in sub-par, often vastly-underperforming, inner city schools. Opposing such alternatives is a repugnant limit to a parent's basic freedom. Yet, the unions and their political handmaidens, like the mayor of New York City, persist. It's noteworthy that the 2014 midterm election was a great victory for educational reform—despite the $100 million teachers' unions spent trying to deceive voters that reformers were "bent on cutting education spending". The unions were crushed in Congressional and governors' races. The same week, however, liberal NYC Mayor de Blasio appointed 15 new school superintendents, all of them union members and half of them principals of failing schools.

Racial justice. As we've tried to show, liberal policies such as minimum wage increases hurt young blacks more than any other group (similarly, one could probably argue that Social Security discriminates against older black males whose average life expectancy is 5.4 years shorter than white Americans', even after significant gains in recent years). As the tragic case of Trayvon Martin shows, the erstwhile leaders of Black Americans have grown seriously out of touch with their constituents. More and more Black Americans have a very different perspective on their needs and status than Jesse Jackson or Al Sharpton would have you believe. Black Americans desperately need better representation.

Gay marriage. Here's another one that obliges Republican candidates to turn cartwheels to avoid offending the far-right voters who are essential to create a level playing field with the much larger universe of registered Democrats. Really—as some gay friends of ours have declared on their vanity license plate for years—"SOWAT"?

GMOs. I expect to die without meeting anyone who ever got sick after eating GMO food. The 2014 midterm was not kind to the GMO alarmists; they lost referendums in Colorado and Oregon (their second defeat there), bringing to four the states which have rejected the proposed GMO labeling requirement. The truth remains—there's simply no credible scientific evidence to support their claims.

Immigration reform. Let's deal with it soon, but let's deal with it right—and keep thoughts of political gain out of it.

Tax reform. As we've noted, in the U.S. we spend up to $265 billion or more *simply filing and collecting our taxes*—more than some developed countries *raise* in total taxes. This is almost as crazy as the way we spend our taxes. There is a better way—a flat tax.

The list seems endless.

A wise person once said, if you don't know where you want to go, any road will take you there. Today, the government often operates without a budget and little long-range fiscal planning. If it were subject to the same regulatory oversight that American companies must endure from the SEC and others, countless government officials would be in the Big House today. The government's version of "generally accepted accounting principles" bears as much resemblance to GAAP as our golf swings bear to that of Rory McIlroy. That today's "off balance sheet" government liabilities amount to almost $200 trillion—which officials don't admit—is reason enough to put some of them behind bars. So we must acknowledge those future bills and we must adopt "generational accounting" with it to show clearly the bill we're running up on future generations.

That would build consensus. Then we can get on with change.

Such change won't happen overnight. But let's make officials set explicit goals for progress along the way. It's what any truly honest office-seeker with managerial experience (there's a near oxymoron) would do.

The easiest challenge we face is fixing Social Security. The answer in part is to conform eligibility to our increasing lifespans and to introduce over time means testing—i.e., if you don't need it, you don't get it—while preserving access for that subset of recipients who are legitimately disabled.

Fixing our healthcare challenge is the big one. As we noted, our aging population is rapidly boosting the gravity of this challenge, at the same time healthcare costs are rising rapidly. Some of this is actually terrific news, as new treatments and drugs are extending lives and improving our well-being. Encouraging innovations like Health Savings Accounts, and incentivizing people to adopt them, will help in many ways, but especially by putting the power of the checkbook in the hands of the consumer—the only approach to cost containment that we haven't tried at any meaningful scale and the one most likely to actually work. Other steps promise outsize benefits:

- 30 percent of Medicare outlays are either wasted or do nothing to improve patient well-being. Let's find them and eliminate them. Forecast savings: billions.
- Fraud is estimated to take 30 percent of Medicare and Medicaid spending and analysts suggest that every dollar spent in ferreting out this waste brings back $8 in recovery. Let's unleash the dogs of war. Forecast savings: billions.
- Stop the plaintiff bar. It's politically tricky (according to the Tort Reform Association, the plaintiff bar gave $60 million to opponents of tort reform between 1988 and 1996—chump change relative to the incredible award of $20 billion in legal fees alone collected from the tobacco litigation). Overwhelmingly, these funds went to Democratic candidates. Putting some constraints on the ambulance chasers would do us a world of good. Corporate chieftains must take their direction from the courageous example of Chevron, which recently triumphed in a mammoth investor-financed suit, and stop "settling" with these plaintiffs and instead fight their actions all the way. Forecast savings from a "loser pays" provision (where, if the plaintiff loses, he pays the defendants' legal bill, a powerful constraint on frivolous litigation that is a basic feature of British law): billions.

Somehow, we must cut the burdensome plethora of government regulations that serve little purpose, but inevitably prove self-perpetuating. They are economic cholesterol and they're killing our prospects for growth. According to the National Association of Manufacturers, the aggregate cost on the American people of federal regulations is $2.028 trillion—that's roughly 12 percent of GDP, or $19,564 per manufacturing employee! No one can plausibly insist that all these regulations serve a valid purpose. And it isn't just federal regulations that must be rationalized. As we've shown, the states can be even more difficult.

We've got to punish the guilty. We've got every right to be furious with those officials who've led us into this box canyon—and have yet to acknowledge it, much less propose sane remedies. We've got to vote against the double-talkers and the hypocrites.

Finally, we must parse the rich cultural endowment we share to revision America so we can all—black/white, rich/poor, liberal/conservative, male/female, gay/straight—believe in her again.

It's Up to You Now

*Every man views the limits of the world through
the limits of his own vision.*

—Schopenhauer

I first saw this book as sort of like another one—Stewart Brand's *Whole Earth Catalog*. Published first in 1968 for $4 a copy, it was an iconic guide to the counterculture's tools; you'll pay $699 to get one from Amazon today. It helped the Sixties generation to build a certain "back to the earth" lifestyle. With this book, I want to do something similar for another generation—to show a path back to the real America we lost along the way.

Grave though our plight may be, we have much to be grateful for.

Not least, as we have hopefully shown by quoting many of them, is the abundance of smart, concerned citizens who reach out to enlighten and serve the rest of us.

The list is long. A fundamental goal of this book has been to introduce you to some of these remarkable people. Some of their books are listed at the end of this one.

It will be said that the central bias of *Turning Point* is conservative, but that would be wrong. The bias on these pages is to what we've found *works*—versus what does not. The smartest voices in the debate about our future share that bias.

To them, we owe a great debt.

We are also owe much to the innovators—those risk-taking folks who together explain why never in the history of man have so many lived so well.

- Our lifespans grow longer each year.
- Infant mortality declines every year.
- Literacy rates grow.
- And poverty goes down.

And, too, as Robert Bryce cites in *Smaller Faster Lighter Denser Cheaper*:

- Many natural resources are, in fact, getting Cheaper. ... (and) we are wringing more and more value out of the energy that we consume.
- Thanks to better agricultural techniques (Author's Note: including GMOs), we are producing more food.
- Today, women are freer and better educated than ever before.

Bryce concludes his remarkable book with these words:

"For decades—even for centuries—we've been deadened by the drumbeat of despair. It's time to dismiss the Jeremiahs who are claiming that our redemption lies in rejecting modernity and economic growth. It's time to reject the dystopians, catastrophists, fear mongers and doomsayers. It's time for an anti-neo-Malthusian outlook. It's time for an outlook that embraces humanism, optimism, technology, and a belief that things are getting better. Such an outlook is not only life-affirming, it also has the virtue of being true. Technology and economic growth have brought—and are bringing—tens of millions of people out of the dark and into the electric-lit world of ideas, education, and fuller, healthier, freer, more fulfilling lives."

All around us we are beset by People With An Agenda. *Their agenda.* Most of the time, it's not our agenda. America has become clotted by special interests of every kind—including our own. This book has tried to get behind their often-feigned concern for your well-being to reveal their cloaked self-interest, even their delusional thinking as well.

Like Bob Dylan once said, all of the people are right part of the time, and a few of the people are right all of the time, but some of the people just aren't all right.

Come to know who the bad guys are and beware their blandishments— especially in election years—like the one that approaches in 2016.

You younger Americans are a remarkable group. You will change the world—for the better. But, with all due respect, you must get to work and sharpen your focus and see your heroes and erstwhile leaders clearly.

And show up.

Many take heart from the 2014 mid-term elections, sensing a turn in our dysfunctional public life. The news was not all good, though. 43 percent of Millennials voted Republican (up from 37 percent in 2012), restoring a little balance and reflecting most suppose their disillusionment with Obama—but only 36.5 percent of eligible voters turned out—which hardly yielded a resounding plebiscite. And the low turnout was due to three key, usually leftward-leaning groups staying home: single women, minorities, and—note carefully—Millennials. You, as a group, were especially apathetic, making up only 14 percent of the vote last fall (versus 19 percent in 2012—itself a decline from two years before).

This won't do. Your future—and the country's—is on the line.

You must do better.

We must each face up to the biggest issue of our time—the choice between a society in which we relinquish ever more power to government, local, state and federal, for more and more decisions over our lives—or we reaffirm the values that have endowed America from its beginning and propelled our success. Chief among those values is the primacy of individual freedom and responsibility.

Our country's remorseless slide into the quick sand of rising but sometime counter-productive entitlements and an ever-bigger, less-effective government has gone on for decades. It will take time to slow this decline—and time is not something we Boomers have much more of. You Millennials do, though.

So let us begin.

Unlike your parents, you idealistic young haven't lived long enough to see good intentions go bad—as we Boomers have, countless times. But your fundamental idealism and your intelligence—aided by unprecedented access to information via technology, which you understand and exploit far more skillfully that we do—fill this writer with optimism.

We did our best, but we came up short.

It's your turn now.

Bibliography

Aftermath: The Unintended Consequences Of Public Policies
by Thomas E. Hall (Cato Institute)

An Inquiry into the Nature and Causes of the Wealth of States: How Taxes, Energy, and Worker Freedom Change Everything by Arthur B. Laffer, Stephen Moore, Rex H. Sinquefield and Travis H. Brown (Wiley)

Handbook for Policy Makers, Cato Institute

Dismantling America by Thomas Sowell (Basic Books)

Economics in One Lesson by Henry Hazlitt (Laissez-Fair Books)

Money Mischief by Milton Friedman (Harcourt Brace)

Please Stop Helping Us: How Liberals Make it Harder for Blacks to Succeed by Jason Riley (Encounter)

The Road To Serfdom by F.A.Hayek (University of Chicago Press)

Restoring Financial Sanity: How to Balance the Budget, edited by Alice M. Rivlin and Isabel Sawhill (Brookings Institution Press)

Return To Prosperity by Arthur Laffer And Stephen Moore (Simon and Schuster)

Running On Empty by Peter G. Peterson (St. Martin's Press)

The Secret Knowledge by David Mamet (Sentinel/Penguin)

Smaller, Faster, Lighter, Denser, Cheaper by Robert Bryce (Perseus Books)

Tradeoffs by Harold Winter (Chicago)

Who's The Fairest Of Them All?—The Truth About Opportunity, Taxes And Wealth In America by Stephen Moore (Encounter Books)

Why Government Is The Problem by Milton Friedman (Hoover Institution Press)

Figures

Index

CPSIA information can be obtained at www.ICGtesting.com
Printed in the USA
BVOW02s2044020915

416324BV00003B/4/P

9 780692 464786